The Christian COOKBOOK

A collection of recipes for home and parish use

compiled by

FÉLICITÉ NESHAM
and
HELEN KILMINSTER

with illustrations by
Barbara Cooper

MOWBRAY
LONDON & OXFORD

Copyright © Félicité Nesham, 1980

ISBN 0 264 66735 2

First Published in 1980 by
A.R. Mowbray & Co. Ltd,
Saint Thomas House, Becket Street,
Oxford, OX1 1SJ.

All rights reserved. No part of this publication may be reproduced, stored in a retrieval system, or transmitted, in any form or by any means, electronic, mechanical, photocopying, recording, or otherwise, without the prior permission in writing from the publisher, A.R. Mowbray & Co. Ltd.

Typeset by O.L.P. Graphics, Oxford.

Printed in Great Britain by Stott Brothers Ltd, Halifax.

Contents

		page	
	Introduction	page	5
	Acknowledgements		6
1	ADVENT		7
2	CHRISTMAS DINNER		11
3	SHROVE TUESDAY and LENT		15
	Carnival		15
	Shrove Tuesday		17
	Lenten Lunches		19
	Mothering Sunday		20
	Palm Sunday		22
	Good Friday		22
4	EASTER		26
5	ASCENSION, WHITSUN (or PENTECOST) and TRINITY SUNDAY		30
	Ascension Day		30
	Whitsunday		31
	Trinity Sunday		33
6	SUMMER DAYS		34
	Picnics and Outings		34
	Church Fetes		37
7	MICHAELMAS		43
8	HARVEST SUPPER		46
9	PARISH CATERING		50
	Stewardship Suppers		50
	The Parish Breakfast		52

10	**SPECIAL SUNDAYS and Other Feasts**	54
	Bible Sunday	54
	New Year's Day	55
	Patronal Festival	55
	Overseas Sunday	56
	Confirmation Sunday	58
	Any Sunday	59
11	**SAINTS' DAYS**	60
	Saint Valentine	60
	Saint Denis	61
	Saint Luke	62
	Patron Saints of the British Isles	63
	Appendix	68
	Metric Conversion Table	69
	Index of Recipes	70

Introduction

Our ancestors lived by two calendars: the succession of the seasons, with the ripening fruits of summer and autumn following the scarcity of winter and spring, and the feasts and fasts of the Christian year. It was natural that church festivals should become associated with the foods that were in season, and that certain dishes should acquire a religious significance. Some traditions linger only in ancient recipe books and old people's memories and the reasons for others seem to be forgotten, but new ones are coming into being, either on a parochial scale, with such events as the Lenten Lunch and Harvest Supper, or in individual families, celebrating a Saint's day or a special Sunday. In the following pages you will find recipes and suggestions that will not only enable you to cook through the Christian year as your grandmothers did, but to establish new traditions of your own.

Down Ampney with Poulton Vicarage F.N. and H.K.
Gloucestershire

ACKNOWLEDGEMENTS

Recipes are rather like prayers: some are so long established that they have become universal property, although the wording may change here and there; others still go by the names of the people who first composed them. Most of the recipes in this book are of the former kind and we have collected them from too many varied sources to be able to acknowledge them all individually. We would, however, like to thank our friends and relations, both here and overseas, who have offered suggestions and recipes, and to express our gratitude to the following: Mrs Elspeth Newton, of Ontario, and the Canadian Mothers' Union for the story of and the recipe for Queen Victoria's Christmas pudding; Dawn MacLeod for her tansy pudding from 'A Book of Herbs' (Duckworth); the Devon and Gloucestershire Women's Institutes for ideas from the 'Devon W.I. Cookbook' and 'Gleanings from Gloucestershire Housewives'; and the 'Farmers Weekly', whose book 'Farmhouse Fare', currently published by the Hamlyn Publishing Group, is a treasurehouse of tradition. We are also indebted, as least for inspiration, to Mrs Beeton and to 'Tried Favourites', by her lesser-known Scottish counterpart, Mrs Kirk.

It is even more difficult to trace the sources and the means of verifying the traditions and stories connected with the recipes. They vary from anonymous, undated newspaper cuttings tucked into old recipe books to the 1894 edition of Dr E. Brewer's invaluable and utterly fascinating 'Dictionary of Phrase and Fable', published by Cassell & Co. Others are 'The English Festivals' by Laurence Whistler (Heinemann 1947), various Books of Saints, dictionaries and encyclopaedias and verbal traditions in our own and other families. We are also grateful to Methuen and Co. for permission to quote from 'Wine, Water and Song' by G.K. Chesterton.

1. Advent

'The collect,' announced the priest, 'for the Sunday next before Advent: "Stir up, O Lord, the wills of thy faithful people..." ' and our grandmothers, heads devoutly bowed over clasped, gloved hands, thought:

'"Stir up Sunday": I must make my Christmas puddings.'

The puddings made one Advent were, of course, usually eaten the following Christmas, but the collect served as a useful reminder: the Church's Year had completed its full cycle and it was time to begin again.

Too many cooks may spoil the broth but Christmas puddings somehow go better when many hands are involved and, for children, making puddings is really more fun than eating them. You can get to nibble quite a lot of sticky, tasty things while the ingredients are chopped and mixed together and when all the members of the family take turns to stir the pudding and make a wish (which mustn't be told!) there is an expectancy in the air which says: 'Christmas is coming!'

Many families have their own traditional recipes, but the following from Canada has an impeccable pedigree and an interesting story attached. It would be worth trying and adopting as your own, especially if you have never made one before.

Queen Victoria's Christmas Pudding

In 1912, in Manitoba, Canada, a woman who had worked in the kitchens of Buckingham Palace as a girl gave a treasured recipe to a young bride for a wedding present. This was known as 'Queen Victoria's Christmas pudding' and many years later the recipient's daughter began making puddings according to this recipe (with the addition of candied pineapple) with her Mothers' Union Branch of St James's, Guelph, Ontario. These are sold to raise funds for the Missionary Dioceses Families Holiday Scheme, chiefly for clergy families from the Arctic.

There is a three or four hour session of tremendous fun, mixing the puddings (in church!) and then they are taken to various homes to be cooked — about 130 lbs of them. The majority are ordered in advance but there seems to be no difficulty in disposing of any left over, even at inflated, fund-raising prices.

Ingredients *for 10 lbs of pudding. The recipe can be halved or increased.*

½ lb flour (two 8 oz cups)
1 lb grated suet
½ lb breadcrumbs (two 8 oz cups)
1 lb sultanas
1 lb seedless raisins
1 lb currants
½ lb crystallized cherries
½ lb candied pineapple
grated rind and juice of two lemons
½ lb almonds, blanched and chopped
¾ lb mixed peel
½ lb granulated sugar (one 8 oz cup)
½ lb soft brown sugar — NOT demerara sugar
6 eggs, well-beaten
2 large apples, peeled and chopped
4 tablespoons orange marmalade
2 tablespoons light molasses
2 tablespoons each: salt, cinnamon, mace and nutmeg
2 wineglasses brandy (4 or 5 oz)

Method

Combine dry ingredients and fruit, plus grated lemon rind. Then add eggs, juice, molasses and marmalade. Mix well and add brandy. Steam or simmer in boiling water in well-buttered pudding bowls covered with double thickness of buttered wax paper and a cloth. Cook 1 and 1½ lb puddings for four hours before storing, larger puddings for up to six hours. You can't really over-cook as long as the pan doesn't go dry. A covered roasting pan in a medium oven does several at a time.

Mince Pies and Punch

Only a strict traditionalist objects to carols in Advent these days and you have to be a real Scrooge not to be moved by the sound of voices on the frosty air outside the house raised, more or less tunefully, in 'The First Nowell' or 'Once in Royal'. Carol-singing is now often an organised affair as the W.I., the Brownies and the church choir come round collecting for a charity and, if it is known in advance that they are coming, they can be welcomed with the seasonal refreshment of mince pies and punch.

Mince pies are as much a part of Christmas fare as turkey and plum pudding but today it seems largely forgotten that they were originally oval in shape to represent the Manger, with three holes pricked in the pastry lid for the Three Wise Men, the rich mincemeat being their gifts. Children still attempt to eat twelve before New Year's Day to ensure twelve happy months, which can be quite a feat with all the other Christmas goodies to ingest as well. It would be easier to try to consume twelve before Twelfth Night on January 6th and perhaps this was the original idea.

Recipes for mincemeat seem generally to consist of equal quantities of apples, raisins, currants, sugar and suet, plus candied fruits, spices and sherry or brandy in varying amounts. Mrs Beeton suggests a quarter pint of the latter and actually includes meat: '½ lb of raw lean beef' to approximately 1 lb of each of the other main ingredients, although she does add that many people prefer it without. She goes on to say that mincemeat needs to be made at the beginning of December so, unless you are planning well in advance, it probably is simplest to buy your mincemeat ready made in jars.

In the Fen district mince pies are eaten all the year round but the Christmas ones sometimes have lids of icing sugar to make them special.

Ingredients *for two dozen mince pies*

1 lb self-raising flour	*for iced pies*
4 oz margarine	2 oz icing sugar
4 oz lard	few drops water
½ teaspoon salt	
¾ lb mincemeat	
water	

Method

Sieve flour and salt into mixing bowl. Cut fat into small pieces and rub into flour with tips of fingers and thumbs until it looks like breadcrumbs. Mix in as little cold water as possible with a knife blade until a stiff dough is formed. Place dough on a floured board and cut twenty-four rounds (if you can't manage ovals!) 3 ins in diameter and twenty-four 2½ ins in diameter. Line greased patty tins with the larger rounds and fill centres with mincemeat. Dampen edges of pastry with cold water, cover with smaller rounds and press edges together. Make a small slit (or three small slits) in the centre of each pie with the point of a knife, brush with a little cold water and sprinkle with caster sugar. Cook in the centre of moderate oven (350°F; gas mark 4) for 20-25 minutes.

Iced Pies

Use half the above quantities of flour, margarine and lard and proceed with recipe cutting twenty-four base rounds only. Fill with mincemeat and bake as above. Mix icing sugar with a few drops of water and spread over mincemeat when cool.

Punch

The name 'Punch' comes from the Hindustani word 'panch', meaning 'five' as it should consist of five ingredients and Dr Brewer, in his 'Dictionary of Phrase and Fable', says it is also called 'Contradiction' because it contains *'spirits* to make it *strong* and *water* to make it *weak, lemon juice* to make it *sour* and *sugar* to make it *sweet'*. The fifth ingredient is spice. A less expensive alternative which, with its five ingredients, can also claim to be a Punch may well be preferred, especially if the carol singers are very young.

Ingredients

1 bottle orange squash
2 bottles fizzy lemonade
1 bottle cider (apple juice may be used if preferred)
1 orange
1 apple

Method

Pour all the liquid into a large bowl and stir well. Thinly slice the orange and cut each slice in half. Peel and core apple and cut into thin slices. Float orange and apple slices in liquid. This punch is better for standing and, if possible, should be made at least six hours in advance. The amount and strength of the cider used can be varied according to the age and tastes of those who are to drink it.

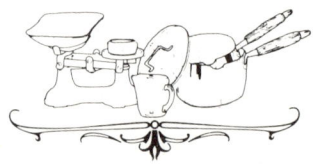

2. Christmas Dinner

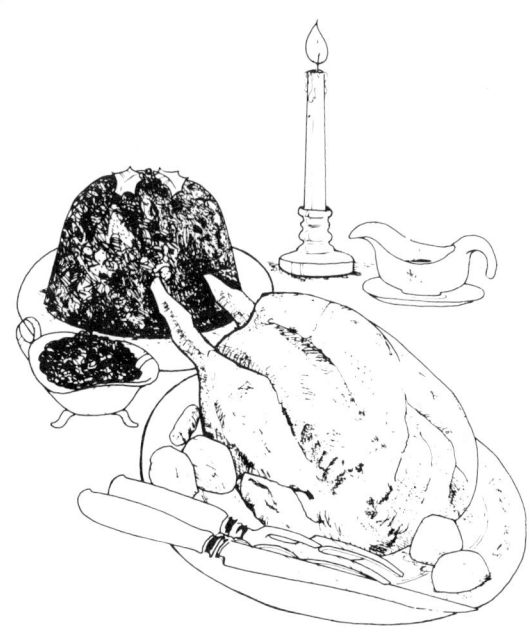

It always seems unfair that the person who would benefit most from the rest and refreshment of church on Christmas morning is the one person least likely to be there — she will be too busy cooking the dinner. The following timetable, with recipes, has been worked out to allow her two hours on Christmas morning when she will be free to go to church with her family. It will, of course, have to be adapted to fit in with the times of the service in her local church, distance to be travelled, her own particular requirements, etc, but, basically, there are two hours during which the dinner can be left to itself, even without an automatic oven.

Suggested Menu

Roast turkey (approx 13 lb) with *either* sausage meat and celery, apple and onion stuffing *or* chestnut and sausagemeat stuffing
Roast potatoes
Roast parsnips
Sprouts
Frozen peas
Cranberry sauce, bread sauce, gravy
Christmas pudding and brandy butter
Mince pies
Arctic roll

We begin, of course, on CHRISTMAS EVE.

1. Make *stuffing*, and stuff turkey. Place in baking dish with dripping, and cover with foil.

Celery, Onion and Apple Stuffing

Ingredients

2 medium onions, chopped
2 oz dripping
4 sticks celery, chopped
1 large cooking apple, diced
4 oz breadcrumbs

2 teaspoons mixed herbs
1 teaspoon caster sugar
salt and pepper to taste
a little stock

Method

Fry the onion in dripping in a saucepan until tender. Add the celery, cook for a few minutes, add diced apple. Stir well, then remove from heat, add breadcrumbs, herbs, sugar and seasoning. Toss well together, add a little stock only if the mixture seems very dry as apples and celery will moisten during cooking.

Chestnut and Sausagemeat Stuffing

Ingredients

1 lb chestnuts (or tin chestnut purée)
liver of turkey
dripping
3 small onions
1 lb pork sausage meat

¼ pint stock or chestnut water
1 tablespoon chopped parsley
1 teaspoon mixed herbs
grated rind of ½ lemon
2 oz white breadcrumbs

Method

Shell chestnuts, boil until tender, add liver and simmer for five minutes. Drain, and save stock. Mince chestnut and liver mixture to a paste. (If using chestnut purée, boil liver in a little water for five minutes, drain and save liquid. Mince liver, and mix into paste with purée.) Fry chopped onions until soft, add to the chestnut and liver mixture along with sausage meat. Mix to a moist consistency with stock, or chestnut and liver water, add parsley, herbs, lemon rind and breadcrumbs. Season to taste. Mix well.

2. Make *bread sauce*

Ingredients

2 oz breadcrumbs
½ teaspoon salt
½ pint milk

1 small onion
2 cloves
½ oz butter (to be added next day)

Method

Stick cloves into onion and put into milk. Simmer for 15 minutes. Strain the milk over breadcrumbs and add seasoning. Just before serving, add butter and re-heat.

3. Peel *sprouts* and *parsnips* and place in cold water. Cover.*
4. Peel *potatoes*, parboil, strain and leave covered.*
5. Make *brandy butter*.*

*These jobs can be done by any visitor unwary enough to say: 'Can I help?'

Brandy Butter

Ingredients

2 oz butter
1 tablespoon brandy
4 oz caster sugar

Method

Cream butter and sugar until soft, add brandy and mix well. Refrigerate until needed.

6. The *Christmas puddings* and *mince pies* have, of course, been made already (see Advent, pages 8 and 9) but many children do not like this traditional fare. *Arctic Roll*, obviously Father Christmas's staple diet, provides an easy alternative which can be made beforehand. It is simple and safe enough for the children to make themselves, and could be an ideal way of occupying them during some of those unending hours before they can hang up their stockings.

Arctic Roll

Ingredients

1 lb crushed sweet biscuits
2 oz chopped nuts
2 oz glacé cherries (chopped)
2 oz marshmallows
2 oz coconut
small tin evaporated milk

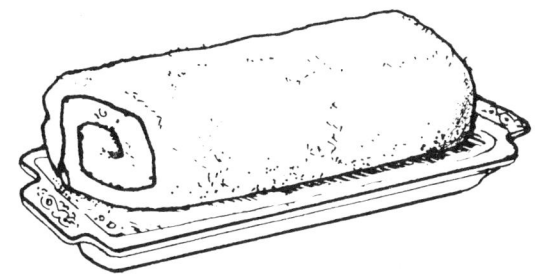

Method

Mix all ingredients together, except for coconut. Place on a pastry board and form into a roll. Sprinkle with coconut until roll is completely covered with a thin coat. Wrap in greaseproof paper and put in refrigerator until set (at least one hour). When needed, remove greaseproof paper, slice and serve.

And so on to CHRISTMAS DAY.

The following timetable allows the cook two hours for church between ten and twelve. It can be adapted according to local circumstances.

8.45 a.m.	Set oven 350°F (180°C) gas mark 4.
9.00	Place turkey on floor of oven.
9.30	Put sprouts on to boil. (If preferred sprouts can be boiled quickly on top of stove after church.)
	Roll potatoes in seasoned flour.
	Wrap frozen peas in tinfoil with a pat of butter.
10.00	Place potatoes and parsnips around turkey.
	Place sprouts in covered casserole in boiling water and place in oven.
	Place peas in oven.
	Interval for church.
12 noon	Boil kettle, put water in steamer with Christmas pudding.
	Put butter in bread sauce and place in oven to warm.
	Make gravy (thin brown for turkey).
	Put plates and dishes to warm.
1.00 p.m.	Serve dinner.
	(Cranberry sauce can be bought ready made. If homemade is preferred it should be done on Christmas Eve.)
	Turn oven to lowest heat and put mince pies to warm while eating the first course.

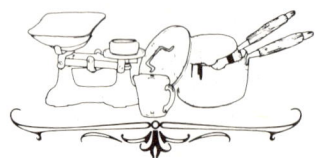

3. Shrove Tuesday and Lent

Carnival

And so from the feast of Christmas to the fast of Lent. But first, Carnival — 'farewell to meat' — still celebrated in some countries in the traditional way at the traditional time. In England we seem to have transferred the word from the feast to the festivities that went with it, and a carnival is now a civic jollification, usually in the summer. But, whatever we call it, couldn't a pre-Lent supper be a good excuse for a Parish get-together? Elsewhere in this book there are recipes for large scale catering (Harvest and Stewardship Suppers, pages 46 and 50) but this is surely the place for a Creole Recipe for Mardi Gras Salad: to be eaten presumably with the fat bulls that were paraded through the streets on Shrove Tuesday before being slaughtered.

Mardi Gras Salad

Ingredients *for approximately twelve people*

½ cup French dressing
6 tablespoons mayonnaise
2 lbs cooked potatoes, diced
4 hardboiled eggs, chopped
½ cup cooked carrots, diced
½ cup string beans
1 red pepper
½ green pepper
½ lb cheese, grated
1 chopped onion
3 tablespoons chopped parsley
2 teaspoons salt
lettuce
radishes

Method

Blend dressing and mayonnaise. Add potatoes and eggs and allow to stand for ten to fifteen minutes. Add green pepper, cheese, onion, parsley and salt. Mix well. Put in salad bowl to chill. Toss well. Garnish with strips of red pepper and lettuce. Fill the centre with radish roses or string beans and diced carrots.

Brisket of Beef

Mardi Gras or, literally, 'Fat Tuesday' refers to the bulls that were killed for consumption before the fast of Lent. In these days lean meat is preferred and a good lean brisket of beef, boned and rolled by the butcher, is an economical joint, ideal for a Parish Carnival or pre-Lent Supper as it can be served hot or cold with a sauce made from its own stock.

Ingredients *for approximately twelve people*

5-6 lb lean brisket, boned and rolled
dripping
spices
seasoning

Method

Spread brisket with a little made mustard and season with salt, pepper, mixed spice and cooking herbs as desired. Cook on top of stove with a little dripping till brown on all sides. Add a few bay leaves and transfer to a very slow oven for five to six hours. Drain off liquid into a bowl and set aside. Put beef onto a dish and press with weights on another dish on top. Slice when cool.

Sauce

Ingredients

2 teaspoons made mustard
2 oz butter
3 tablespoons cream
2 tablespoons flour
1 pint stock (from the beef)

Method

Lift dripping* from on top of stock and set aside. Melt the butter and stir in flour. Cook for a few minutes, then add one pint of the stock, stirring all the time. Bring to boil, simmer for two minutes, stir in made mustard and cream. Cool, then refrigerate.

To serve meat hot lay slices in an oven-proof serving dish, pour on about two or three tablespoons stock, cover with foil and heat gently till warmed through. Re-heat sauce, boiling it down to a fairly thick consistency. Just before serving pour over meat, or serve separately in a jug.

To serve meat cold lay slices on a serving dish, or straight onto plates. Put sauce into blender with a little milk and serve separately.

*The dripping can be used to make Irish cake (see page 65) for St Patrick's Day in a few weeks' time.

Shrove Tuesday

Fastnachts

These are an American Shrove Tuesday tradition and make an interesting alternative to pancakes. The following recipe makes four dozen.

Ingredients

2 cups milk
1 oz yeast
6 to 7 cups sifted flour
1 cup sugar
3 eggs, well-beaten

½ teaspoon nutmeg
¼ cup melted butter or other shortening
¼ teaspoon salt
(remember 1 American cup = 8 fl oz)

Method

Scald milk and set aside to cool. Soften yeast with one cup lukewarm water, add half cup of flour and mix to a batter. Add scalded milk when lukewarm. Stir in one teaspoon of the sugar and about three cups of flour. Set in a warm place to rise overnight, or until doubled in bulk. Add the well-beaten eggs, nutmeg, butter, remaining sugar and salt and mix thoroughly. Stir in flour until batter can no longer be stirred with a spoon. Set aside to rise until light. Roll on a well-floured board and cut into rounds. Let rise again and fry in deep hot fat (370°F) until brown.

Pancakes

However, for most English people *Shrove Tuesday*, so-called because it was customary for people to be shriven, or to receive absolution for their sins after confession before Lent began, nowadays means pancakes — traditionally eaten on this day to use up the butter and eggs in the larder before the Lenten fast. Few people do this seriously today — unless they are using Lent to stiffen their resolution to diet — but most people still toss their pancake. If wanted for a Carnival Supper the required quantity can be made beforehand and kept in a freezer until needed. The basic recipe is simple.

Ingredients *for 16-20 pancakes*

8 oz plain flour
2 eggs
1 oz melted butter

1 pint milk
pinch of salt
a little melted butter for cooking

Method

1. Sift the flour and salt into a bowl and make a well in the centre.
2. Break eggs, one at a time, into a cup and drop into the well with half a cup of the milk.
3. Begin mixing the eggs rapidly with a wooden spoon so that the flour comes in from the sides of the well. Take care to keep the mixture smooth. Gradually add up to half the remainder of the milk, beating thoroughly until all the flour is incorporated and the mixture like a thick cream. Add the rest of the milk, stirring carefully so as not to remove the air.
4. Stir in the melted butter.

(Stages 1—4 can just as easily be done in a liquidiser, following the maker's instructions.)

5. Cover, and leave in a cool place for at least half-an-hour, preferably for three to four hours, to allow to develop.
6. Cook the pancakes by brushing a small amount of melted butter over a good thick flat frying pan. Make sure it is hot before putting in the mixture. Then pour in a good tablespoon of the batter, sufficient to cover the bottom of the pan thinly. (If you tip the pan, pour in the batter at the edge and roll quickly round the pan, you get an even coating.) Cook over a fairly high heat until brown underneath (about one minute) shaking the pan to keep the pancake loosened. Toss, or turn with a broad-bladed palette knife and cook on the other side for about the same length of time.

If wanted for freezer: Spread pancakes out on plates or a formica-topped table to cool, turning frequently and wiping away moisture left by warm pancake. Make a stack of pancakes, separating each layer with a sheet of greaseproof paper. Freeze flat in polythene bags. *To thaw*, remove from freezer about two hours before they are needed. Separate, fold when thawed and lay on a greased baking sheet. Cover with foil and heat through (about twenty minutes in a hot oven).

To keep pancakes hot: If you are cooking a number of pancakes for immediate consumption you have, in a way, the opposite problem: how to keep the first ones hot until the rest are cooked. This is one way: place an upturned saucer on a dinner plate and put the pancakes as they are cooked, one on top of another, on top of the saucer, cover with a tea towel and keep in a warm place. When the required number have been cooked they can all be filled and served at the same time. (The upturned saucer raises them slightly in the middle, making it easier to peel them off.)

To serve: Sprinkle with lemon juice and caster sugar. A savoury or sweet filling can be used instead, if desired.

Savoury: Minced, cooked meat, lightly browned chopped onions, seasoning, a little stock to bind; grated cheese; cooked rice, mixed diced vegetables; mushrooms; tomatoes; etc.

Sweet: Stewed fruit, with custard poured over; jam; syrup.

And here is a Special: you will need that Lenten fast after this one.
Spread a pancake with warmed jam. Sprinkle with grated chocolate and icing sugar. Place another pancake on top and repeat until you have the required number. Sprinkle icing sugar only on the top one, cut in sections and serve with chocolate sauce.

Lenten Lunches

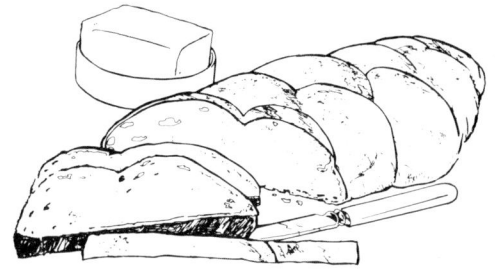

The austerity lunch is a new dimension of the Lenten fast: a tradition in the making perhaps. Many parishes and other Christian organisations provide a soup and bread-and-cheese lunch on a weekday in Lent at an inflated price, donating the profits to a good cause, usually a Third World charity. Fresh homemade bread is always welcome at these lunches, although admittedly it can turn a fast into a feast.

There is something very satisfying about making your own bread. It is not the thought that the word 'lady' derives from the Angol-Saxon 'hlaef-dige' or 'loaf-kneader' so that you can feel superior as you thump at the dough, nor the achievement when the sticky mess becomes a smooth, pliable dough. Perhaps it just is that bread is the staff of life and there is something rather special about it. Country women used to murmur a prayer as they worked the dough and make the mark of a cross in the flour scattered over the yeast mixture, 'to prevent the fairies dancing on it'.

The following recipe, in which all times and quantities should be preceded by the word 'about', makes six loaves, approximately 2 × 7 inches.

Homemade Bread

Ingredients

3 lb strong plain flour: 81%, 85% or 100% extraction, obtainable at Whole Food Stores, where you can also get *granary* flour, which makes a malty loaf, delicious with cheese.
1 dessertspoonful salt
1½ pints liquid (¼ pint milk, 1¼ pints water is a good mixture)
1 tablespoonful sugar, preferably brown, or honey
2 tablespoonfuls cooking oil, or margarine
1 oz yeast. Fresh yeast can be obtained as above, or from bakeries. Made up into 1 oz packets, it keeps well in the deep freeze. Thaw before using. Dried yeast can be used.

Method

Put flour into large mixing bowl and add salt. If using margarine, rub into flour. Put yeast into small bowl and add honey or sugar, stirring till yeast liquefies. Heat milk to boiling point and add to cold water, to produce luke-warm liquid. If using oil, add to liquid and pour half a pint onto yeast. Make a 'well' in the flour and pour in yeast mixture, or 'barm'. Cover surface with a light scattering of flour and leave for fifteen minutes. This is called 'laying leavens'. Mix barm into the rest of the flour, adding remaining liquid slowly, mixing in all the flour with your hands. The dough should be of a moist, sticky consistency, with all the flour absorbed. If necessary, add more luke-warm liquid. Alternatively, you may not need it all. Knead until the dough comes away cleanly from the sides of the bowl and from your fingers — for five to fifteen minutes. Cover with a clean cloth and leave in a warm place until it has approximately doubled in size. This usually takes 1½-2 hours. Push fingers into the dough to let out air, turn onto floured board and knead again. Shape into the required number of loaves and put into greased tins. Put into warm place again, covered with a cloth, for a further twenty minutes. Bake in a hot oven for half-an-hour, or in a very hot oven for fifteen minutes, reducing heat to moderate for further half to three-quarters of an hour. Turn upside down onto a wire tray to cool. Loaves should sound hollow when tapped.

If wanted for an austerity lunch, bring-and-buy sale etc, hide from family.

A recipte for bread rolls in included in Chapter 8 (Harvest Supper, page 47).

Mothering Sunday

'On Mothering Sunday, above all other
Every child should dine with its mother.'

So goes the old rhyme and in recent years we have seen a revival of this custom, although it has inevitably been commercialised and hopelessly confused with the twentieth-century American 'Mother's Day', an entirely secular feast celebrated on the second Sunday in May. The origins of the name, 'Mothering Sunday', are obscure. Some say it is a corruption of 'Mid-Lent Sunday', but it seems just as likely to have come from the medieval practice of all parishes worshipping in the Cathedral, the 'mother' church of the Diocese, on the fourth Sunday in Lent, which in turn can be traced back to pre-Christian times and the honouring by the Jews of the Temple in Jerusalem with a special festival. It was on this Sunday that apprentice boys and girls in service in the big house were given a day off and walked home along country lanes and across fields, picking fistfuls of spring flowers as they went, which they thrust into their mothers' hands at the cottage doors. Sometimes they brought Simnel cakes, sometimes these were baked by the welcoming mothers, who also prepared a dish of frumenty.

There are regional variations of Simnel cake and at least two explanations of its curious name. The learned derive it from the Latin 'simila', 'finest wheat flour', which perhaps has come by way of the Old German, 'semnel', 'a roll, or manchet', as Dr Brewer suggests. Sadly, it seems improbable that the name originated from the making up of a quarrel between one Simon and one Nell as to the best method of cooking it. There is a good deal of significance attached to this cake, traditionally eaten on 'Refreshment Sunday', the other name for the fourth Sunday in the six-week fast of Lent. According to Dr Brewer it reminds us of the feast Joseph prepared for his brothers (Genesis 43, the old Prayer Book lesson for Evensong for that day) as well as the feeding of the five thousand (John 6, the Prayer Book Gospel). Some recipes require its decoration by marzipan balls. These should be eleven in number, in memory of the disciples who remained true to Jesus after his betrayal by the twelfth, Judas Iscariot.

Simnel Cake

Ingredients

for cake: 8 oz flour
             6 oz butter
             6 oz caster sugar
             4 eggs
             1½ lbs mixed raisins, sultanas, currants, peel
             ½ teaspoon mixed spice
for paste: ½ lb ground almonds
             4 oz castor sugar
             4 oz icing sugar
             1 egg
             juice of ½ lemon
             alternatively the paste can
             be bought ready made

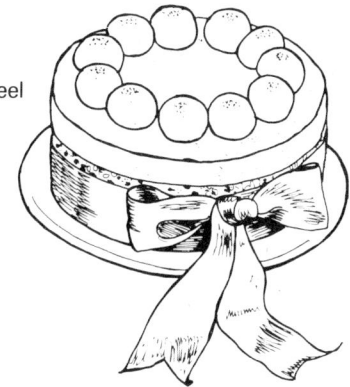

Method

To make the paste, mix ground almonds and both kinds of sugar together, add beaten egg and the lemon juice. Pound to a stiff paste. Turn onto board lightly dusted with icing sugar, divide into two halves and roll out each the size of the cake tin, keeping back a little for decoration.

To make the cake, cream the butter and sugar together until white and creamy. Beat one egg at a time in a cup and add to the mixture with a little flour, beating well after each egg is added. Stir in the rest of the flour and all the fruit and mixed spice thoroughly, but as lightly as possible. Place half the mixture in a well-greased cake tin and smooth flat. Place one layer of almond paste on top and add the remaining cake mixture and cook in a moderate oven for about two hours. When nearly cooked, take out and add second layer of almond paste, mark like a chess-board with a knife, brush with egg or milk and return to oven till cake is quite cooked. Decorate with eleven almond paste balls and, if wished, a little icing sugar and designs suitable for Easter.

Frumenty: Frumety: Fermitty

These are only three of the many different ways of spelling the name of this old English dish, traditionally served at different times of the year in different parts of the country. In Gloucestershire at any rate it was firmly associated with Mothering Sunday, although one does not often meet it nowadays. As most of the recipes seem to begin with phrases such as 'Soak a pint of wheat in spring water for three days' or 'simmer wheat in water until tender — for twenty-four hours or more' this is not surprising. However some Whole Food Stores sell packets of wheat which has already gone through the tenderising, dehusking process and can be considered the same at the 'prepared wheat' of some of the old recipes. This wheat can be used straightaway although it is a little more tender if boiling water is poured on it and it is left to soak overnight.

Ingredients

2 pints milk
¼ lb raisins
¼ lb currants
3 tablespoons flour
1 breakfast cup prepared wheat
¼ grated nutmeg
2 eggs (optional)

Method

Put wheat, currants and rasins into milk and bring to the boil. Thicken with flour, add nutmeg and sweeten to taste. Boil for ten minutes, keeping well stirred, or simmer for about half an hour. If wished, stir in two beaten eggs before serving.

Palm Sunday

The Lenten fast is nearly over now. Palm Sunday, says Dr Brewer, was known as 'Fig Sunday' and figs were eaten on this day to commemorate the story of Zacchaeus, who climbed a fig tree to see Jesus. This seems strange, as, with respect to Dr Brewer, it was a sycamore that Zacchaeus climbed and the families who ate their figs in puddings on Good Friday (page 25) marked Palm Sunday more appropriately with Date Pudding.

Date Pudding

Ingredients

½ lb self-raising flour
4 oz butcher's suet, chopped fine or 3 oz packet suet
4 oz chopped dates
1-4 oz sugar, according to taste (the dates are sweet)
1 egg
pinch of salt
enough milk to bind to a slightly moist consistency (about ¼ pint)

Method

Put dry ingredients into a bowl and add finely-chopped dates. Beat egg with some of the milk and add to other ingredients. Mix well, adding more milk if necessary. Pour into a buttered basin (the mixture should drop slowly from the mixing spoon), cover with greaseproof paper and a pudding cloth and steam for 1½ hours, or cook in pressure cooker, following instructions. Serve with custard sauce.

Good Friday

'One a penny, two a penny,
Hot cross buns,
If you have no daughters,
Give them to your sons:
One a penny, two a penny,
Hot cross buns!'

Hot cross buns are traditionally eaten at breakfast on Good Friday and, curiously enough, if the old rhyme is anything to go by, appear to have been sold, at any rate in towns, by street vendors rather than made at home. Why 'hot *cross*'? Because Christ died on the cross on Good Friday, of course. But petrified buns, marked with a cross, were found in the ruins of Herculaneum, which was overwhelmed by a volcano in A.D. 79 at the same time as Pompeii, and these were not likely to have been baked in a Christian household. Cakes marked with a cross appear to have been eaten at pre-Christian festivals so it seems that the Church has taken over this custom, with so many others and, because a cross has such significance for Christians, the earlier associations have been lost.

Hot Cross Buns

Ingredients *for one dozen*

1 lb plain flour
4 oz margarine
4 oz currants
3 oz caster sugar
1 egg

½ oz yeast
¼ cupful milk
small pinch salt
1 teaspoon spice, or to taste

Method

Put flour, sugar, currants, margarine, spices and salt into a bowl and rub well together. Make a hole in the centre and put in the yeast. Pour over a little of the warm milk, no hotter than your finger can bear. Stir in a little of the flour to set a ferment. Cover with a clean cloth and put in a warm place for half an hour. Add the beaten egg and enough warm milk to form a smooth dough. Put back into the warm place for another half-hour to allow the dough to rise. Turn onto a well-floured board and cut into a dozen pieces. Make them round, and roll them out a little. Place on a greased baking sheet, marking each bun with a deep cross, using the back of a knife. Brush them over with a little milk and sprinkle with sugar. Leave them to rise till double their size (about twenty minutes) and bake in a very hot oven for fifteen minutes.

Fish on Good Friday can be anything from salmon to sardines. The following recipe comes somewhere between the two.

Fish Potato Pie *serves four*

Ingredients

1 lb potatoes
1 yolk of egg
1 oz butter
1 tablespoon grated cheese
seasoning

½ lb white fish (coley is ideal, and inexpensive)
1 hard-boiled egg
white sauce
(4 oz margarine, 4 oz flour, 1 pint milk)
chopped parsley

Method

Boil potatoes and mash them with butter, cheese, seasoning and some of the egg yolk. Turn onto a floured board and mould into a case with a hollow in the centre. Brush with rest of egg yolk and bake on a greased baking tin in a hot oven until golden brown.
Cover fish with a little milk in a pan and cook gently until it begins to flake — about ten minutes.
Melt margarine in a saucepan and blend in flour. Cook for a few minutes and add milk gradually, using the milk the fish was cooked in first and then the rest of the pint, stirring all the time. Bring to boil and stir in flaked fish, chopped hard-boiled egg and seasoning. Pour into potato case, garnish with chopped parsley and serve hot.

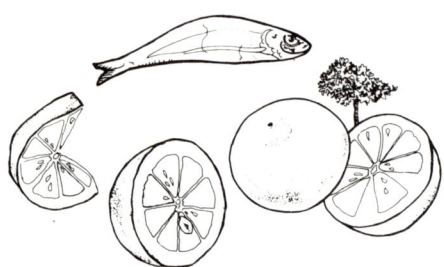

This, or whatever fishy first course is chosen, can be followed by Fig Pudding, a Good Friday tradition with some East Anglian families, which probably had its origin in that strange story of the fig tree, the only destructive miracle performed by Jesus. He had entered Jerusalem in triumph the day before and gone to the Temple, where he drove out the money changers and healed the lame and the blind. He then went out to Bethany for the night and, on his way back to the city in the morning, he felt hungry and, seeing a fig tree by the roadside he went up to it, but found it had no figs.

'May you never bear fruit any more!' he exclaimed and, instantly, says Mark, by the next day, according to Matthew, the fig tree withered.

In both gospels the incident is used as a basis for teaching on faith but, whether it actually happened or not — it may have been a parable told by Jesus, later transformed into an action on his part — it sticks in the mind as something uncharacteristic, but, somehow, very real.

Fig Pudding

Ingredients

4 oz chopped figs
6 oz self-raising flour
3 oz granulated sugar
3 oz fine margarine
1 egg
enough milk to bind to a dropping consistency from a wooden spoon (about ¼ pint)
(Some people use 3 oz suet instead of margarine but, as Good Friday should be a completely meatless day, margarine or any other vegetable shortening is preferable.)

Method

Cream margarine and sugar together. Add beaten egg and some of the milk. Fold in flour and chopped figs, adding milk to the desired consistency. Mix well and turn into a greased basin, cover with greaseproof paper and a pudding cloth and steam for 1½ hours or in pressure cooker, following instructions. Serve with white sauce.

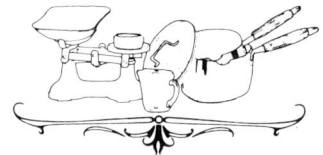

4. Easter

'Easter is eggs' say the Sunday school children firmly, but how many, even in the North of England, still carry on the custom of dyeing and dumping hard-boiled eggs?

Paschal or Pace Eggs

You will need:
1 egg for each child
onion skins and/or non-fast coloured rags
white wax pencil or sharpened candle (optional)

Method

Bind over-lapping onion skins or coloured rags round fresh eggs with rubber bands. If wished, a child's name can be written on each egg first with the wax pencil or pointed candle. This will later show white on the coloured egg. Hard boil the eggs and remove the skins or rags. Rub each shell with a trace of butter to make it shine. Each child then uses the pointed end of his egg to 'dump' another child's egg. The final owner of an un-damaged egg is the winner.

How to wash Mohair Knits

Hand wash in cold water, cool rinse, place in a pillowcase one short spin, dry flat away from direct heat. When dry a light brush will fluff the garment back to life

For the cook, as always, the real business of the day will be the dinner. Perhaps this no longer means roast lamb so inevitably as Christmas means turkey, as the association with the lambs of the Jewish Passover has been forgotten, but it should mean rhubarb tart. There does not seem to be any religious significance for this, unless there is an almost folk-religion feeling that serving the first fruits of any crop at a major Church festival hallows the whole, and certainly rhubarb is very new at Easter. As a change from pastry why not try rhubarb with Dunfillan paste?

Dunfillan Rhubarb serves four

Ingredients

1 lb rhubarb
4 tablespoons flour
3 oz butter
1 egg

1 teaspoon baking powder
2 tablespoon sugar
¼ pint milk
flavouring to taste

Method

Stew rhubarb, preferably with sugar to taste and *no* water in a casserole in a slow oven for about half-an-hour. This can be done in advance. To make the paste, rub the butter into the flour and add baking powder. Beat egg with sugar, add milk and stir all into flour with flavouring (ginger, or nutmeg, or cinnamon etc) to taste. Mix well, and pour over rhubarb and bake in a moderate oven for about half-an-hour.

Rhubarb tart seems to have superseded the once universal Easter pudding: a Tansy. Apparently tansy pudding (and tansy cake) were a traditional part of Easter fare at least until the middle of the last century. Some authorities say the tansy plant represents the bitter herbs of the Passover (which perhaps explains why no one seems to suggest that it was used because people actually liked it) and others, more practical perhaps, point out that it is a stomachic and therefore a useful antidote for the over-eating that followed the Lenten fast. Is it a coincidence, or not, that the word 'tansy' meaning 'an immortal plant' is derived through French and Latin from the Greek 'athanasia: immortality'?

Tansy does not seem to be among the herbs that are readily available in shops. It grows wild on moors and in pastureland in the South of England and we offer the following recipes in case anyone feels inspired to try them.

Tansy Pudding 1 From 'Domestic Cookery' by A Lady (Mrs Rundell)

Ingredients

7 eggs
1 pint cream
1 pint spinach juice
a little tansy juice

¼ lb Naples biscuits
1 glass white wine
some nutmeg
sugar to taste

Method

Beat seven eggs, the yolks and white separately; add a pint of cream, near the same of spinach juice, and a little tansy juice, gained by pounding in a stone mortar, a quarter of a pound of Naples biscuits, sugar to taste, a glass of white wine and some nutmeg. Set all in a saucepan, just to thicken over the fire: then put into a dish lined with paste, to turn out, and bake it.

Tansy Pudding 2 *from 'A Book of Herbs' by Dawn McLeod*

Ingredients

¼ lb Jordan almonds, blanched and pounded
1 gill syrup of roses
some grated nutmeg
2 tablespoons Tansy juice
3 oz fresh butter
some grated lemon

½ glass brandy
1½ pints cream or milk
juice of one lemon
8 beaten eggs
crumbs of a french roll

Method

Mix the crumbs of a french roll with a quarter of a pound of Jordan almonds, blanched and pounded, one gill syrup of Roses, some grated nutmeg, two tablespoons Tansy juice, three ounces fresh butter, some grated lemon, half a glass of brandy. Pour over the mixture one and a half pints of boiling cream or milk, sweetened, and when cold mix it up. Add the juice of a lemon and eight beaten eggs. May be baked or boiled.

Judging by the number of recipes for Easter cakes, biscuits and other goodies our ancestors broke their Lenten fast in no mean way. The two following recipes remind us that other denominations beside our own have their traditions.

Greek Easter Cakes

Ingredients

1 lb flour
6 oz sugar
4 oz warm butter
½ oz yeast
sesame seed
warm water

Method

Mix flour and sugar and pour in warm butter. Knead well, working in yeast dissolved in a little warm water, adding sufficient lukewarm water to make a smooth dough. When thoroughly kneaded, put in a warm place for about two hours for the dough to rise, then roll out on a floured board. Cut into strips and make these into fancy shapes, such as plaits, knots etc. Brush over with sugar moistened with milk and sprinkle with sesame seed. Place on a greased tray and bake in a moderate oven.

The Eastern Orthodox Church traditionally eats Pasca, or Paskha (the word has the same derivation as the Pasch or Pace of the eggs on page 26 from the Jewish Passover) with rich yeast cakes, and the following recipe comes from Russia.

Paskha

Ingredients

4 oz butter or margarine
12 oz cream cheese
5 fl oz sour cream
(or single cream to which a few drops of lemon juice have been added)
4 oz sieved icing sugar

4 oz chopped almonds
4 oz mixed cut peel
4 oz glacé cherries, chopped
4 oz raisins
for decoration: ¼ pint double cream
sugared Easter eggs

Method

Put all ingredients into a bowl and beat with a wooden spoon until smooth. Place in a cylindrical-shaped mould lined with muslin (greaseproof paper will do). Gather muslin together over the top and press mixture well down. Refrigerate until firm. Turn out onto plate. Whip cream and pipe rosettes round the base and decorate with Easter eggs. Slice horizontally.

If you don't feel like tackling the yeast cookery involved in Greek Easter cakes the following is a simple alternative to eat with Paskha.

Easter Biscuits

Ingredients

4 oz butter
4 oz sugar
1 teaspoon mixed spice

8 oz self-raising flour
6 oz currants
a little milk

Method

Cream butter and sugar, fold in flour and spice. Add currants and milk to bind. Roll dough out thinly and cut into large rounds. Put onto a lightly greased baking tray and cook in a moderate oven for 15 to 20 minutes.

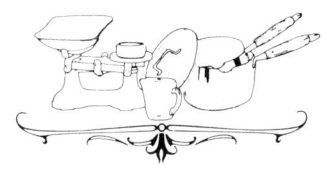

5. Ascension, Whitsun and Trinity Sunday

Ascension Day

The most long-standing tradition must have had a beginning. Why not launch a new one by serving a soufflé on Ascension Day?

Soufflés *for four people*

Ingredients

1 oz butter of margarine	¼ pint milk
1 oz plain flour	3 eggs

Flavouring:

for cheese soufflé: 3 oz finely grated cheese
pinch of salt, mustard, nutmeg, cayenne pepper

for fish soufflé: 4-6 oz finely flaked cooked fish
1 tablespoon lemon juice
pinch of salt, pepper

for chocolate soufflé: 1 oz grated chocolate
1 oz sugar
1 teaspoon vanilla essence
pinch of salt

for lemon soufflé: rind of one lemon (grated)
2 oz sugar
pinch of salt

for vanilla soufflé: 2 oz sugar
1 teaspoon vanilla
pinch of salt

Method

Grease one 2-pint soufflé dish, or four small ones. Melt butter or margarine in a pan and blend in flour. Cook for a few minutes and add milk gradually, stirring all the time. Bring to boil and boil gently for a few minutes. Add egg yolks, beaten with one tablespoon of water, and the flavouring.

(For fish soufflé, the fish and sauce may be rubbed through a sieve or put in blender before adding egg yolks: for chocolate soufflé, dissolve grated chocolate in milk before making suace.) Fold in stiffly beaten egg whites and pour mixture into prepared dish, or dishes. Bake in a moderately hot oven until soufflé is risen and brown (½-¾ hour for a large one. 15-20 minutes for the smaller ones.) Serve at once in the soufflé dish.

Whitsunday

One wonders how our grandmothers managed to make their gooseberry tarts at Whitsun in the years when Easter, and the subsequent festivals, were early, but we, in the deep-freeze age, should have no problems. The following recipe, while not deviating too much from tradition, makes a pleasing variation.

Gooseberry Mallow Pie

Ingredients

4 oz flour	
2 oz margarine	1 lb gooseberries
pinch of salt	14 white marshmallows

Method

Make the pastry as on page 9 (mince pie recipe). Put in a greased flan dish and bake blind in a moderately hot oven for 15-20 minutes. Stew gooseberries slowly, to keep them whole, and cool. (The best way to do this is to put the gooseberries in a casserole with 2-4 oz sugar, cover with lid and cook in a slow oven for 30-40 minutes.) Put gooseberries in pastry case, keeping back a few for decoration. With a pair of wet scissors, cut marshmallows in half horizontally and place in two circles on top of gooseberries, leaving centre free. Place under grill until marshmallows are melting and golden. Fill centre with remaining gooseberries and serve.

For those who prefer a really traditional dish there is only one answer.

Gooseberry Fool *serves four*

Ingredients

1 lb gooseberries
2 - 4 tablespoons sugar
½ pint whipped cream

Method

Cook gooseberries in casserole as on page 31 (gooseberry and mallow pie recipe) and cool. Rub through sieve, preferably nylon, or put in blender. When quite cold, fold pulp into whipped cream and chill thoroughly. Serve very cold.

Another old country dish which appears to be associated with Whitsun, at any rate in Gloucestershire, is 'White Pot' — perhaps because of its name. It also used to be served at village revels and the quantities given in old recipe books are rather daunting. The following scaled down version makes an unusual pudding that can either be served by itself, or as an accompaniment to your gooseberry tart.

White Pot

Ingredients

1 pint milk
2 oz flour
2 oz golden syrup
1 egg
¼ oz butter
¼ grated nutmeg
mixed spice to taste

Method

Beat flour, egg, syrup and spice together. Boil milk and stir it boiling into other ingredients, forming a paste. Pour into a large baking dish and dot pieces of butter on the top. At the last moment pour two fluid ounces of cold water into the middle of the pan and put into a hot oven without stirring. (Cider can be used instead of water). Bake in this oven for about an hour, and then in a cooler oven until set — the old recipes say for a further six to eight hours, but it does not take as long as this! Serve cold.

Trinity Sunday

Curiously enough there do not seem to be any traditional recipes for this Sunday. However, with the ordinations that take place at this season in mind, we offer the following.

Curate's Pudding

Ingredients

3 eggs
their weight in each of the following: butter
                                                       sugar
                                                       flour

Method

Separate the yolks from the white of the eggs and beat well. Beat the butter to a cream, stir in the sugar and the well-beaten egg yolks. Add the flour and the egg whites, beaten to a stiff froth. Put into buttered patty pans and bake immediately for 20 minutes.

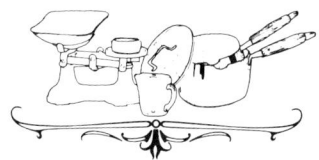

6. Summer Days

Picnics and Outings

The early Church, with the parson farming his glebe and most of the congregation involved in one way or another on the land, seems to have been too busy hay-making and harvesting between Trinity and Michaelmas to have time to celebrate feast days. Those interminable Sundays after Trinity — sometimes now the Sundays after Pentecost — have been referred to, rather desperately, as 'all those green Sundays' after the liturgical colour for the season. Perhaps this is as good an excuse as any for thinking of salads for parish picnics, Mothers' Union outings and Sunday School treats which are among today's Church feasts for this season. Plastic has made the packing of picnic food so much easier than it used to be. Lettuces and tomatoes travel safely in large boxes and cole slaw can be eaten straight from the individual containers in which it is packed.

The following recipes and suggestions are for a packed lunch for a family of four. If you are catering for larger numbers, such as the choir, or the Evergreen Club, double or treble quantities accordingly.

Cole Slaw

Ingredients

1 small white cabbage — this is the basic ingredient
2 small sticks celery
1 medium onion
6 radishes
peppers (enough to add colour)

8 thin slices cucumber
1 handful sultanas
1 handful peanuts
4 tablespoons bean sprouts
2 large tomatoes

Method

Chop all ingredients finely and mix well. Pack into containers. Take dressing in a separate jar or bottle to add at the last minute.

Cole Slaw Dressing

Ingredients

1 dessertspoon sugar
1 dessertspoon flour
1 teaspoon dry mustard
1 teaspoon salt
1 teaspoon butter

½ cup vinegar
½ cup thick cream
yolk of 1 egg
pinch of cayenne pepper

Method

Mix all dry ingredients together with the vinegar in a bowl. Place bowl over saucepan of boiling water and, keeping the water at boiling point, stir mixture until it thickens. Cool for 15 minutes, then add egg, butter and cream and beat thoroughly.
Alternatively, Cole Slaw can be tossed in a mixture of equal parts olive or cooking oil and vinegar, with a pinch of paprika if desired.

Salad Cream (that will keep for months)

Ingredients

1 tablespoon plain flour
1 dessertspoon salt
½ teaspoon pepper
½ tablespoon dry mustard
4 oz sugar

1 egg
1 pint milk
½ pint vinegar
a little vegetable oil

Method

Mix flour, salt, pepper and mustard in a saucepan with the oil to form a smooth paste. Stir in sugar. Stir milk into beaten egg in a bowl and pour into a saucepan, stirring well. Slowly add vinegar, stirring all the time. Bring to boil and simmer until mixture thickens. Cool. Pour into glass jars, seal and store.

Curry Pasties

Once upon a time the Devil, going to and fro in the earth and walking up and down in it, was wandering through England and he came to the River Tamar, the boundary between Devon and Cornwall. An old man was sitting on the bank, fishing, and eating a large pasty.

'That smells good,' said the Devil. 'What is it?'

''Tis a Cornish pasty,' said the old man and took another bite.

The Devil sniffed again.

'What's in it?' he asked.

The old Devonian snorted scornfully. 'They puts everything into un,' he said. 'They would put the Devil in un — if they could catch 'ee!'

Whereupon the Devil gave a loud shriek and disappeared in a cloud of sulphur and brimstone. And that, they say, is why Cornwall is so full of saints: the Devil never crossed the Tamar.

Perhaps a whiff of that sulphur and brimstone got into these curried pasties after all but, in any case, they make a delicious component of a packed lunch.

Ingredient

for pastry: 8 oz flour
4 oz margarine
pinch of salt

for filling: ½ lb cooked minced meat
3 medium cooked carrots
1 large cooked potato
1 large onion
1 meat cube or ¼ pint stock
small knob margarine
2 teaspoons curry powder — for medium flavour.
Use more or less, as preferred
Other vegetables can be used as available

Method

Filling: chop onion finely and fry until tender. Mix with diced carrots and potatoes or other vegetables in a bowl. Dissolve meat cube in ½ cup boiling water, or heat stock. Melt margarine over low heat, remove and stir in curry powder. Return to heat for one minute, stirring all the time, then stir in liquid, add vegetables and meat. Simmer, stirring ocassionally for ¼ hour. Leave to cool.

Pastry: make pastry as on page 9 (mince pie recipe). Roll out dough on floured board and cut out pasties — an average saucer is a good guide for size. Fold each round in half, then open and place flat. Place filling on rounds, keeping to one side of the centre fold line. Damp edge with cold water and fold over, pressing edges firmly together. Place on a greased baking tray, make a small slit in the middle of each pasty, brush with a little milk if a glazed effect is preferred and bake for approximately 20 minutes in a preheated moderate oven.

Cheese, Egg and Onion Flan

This is a tasty alternative for those who don't like curry.

Ingredients

for pastry: 4 oz flour   *for filling:*   2 eggs
               2 oz margarine   1 medium onion
               pinch of salt   2 oz grated cheese
                                                         ½ cup of milk
                                                         1 medium tomato   } optional
                                                         2 small mushrooms

Method

Make the pastry as on page 9 (mince pie recipe), roll out and line a 7 inch, greased sponge tin. Chop onion and fry in a little fat until tender. Strain off fat and put onion in bottom of flan. Whisk eggs in a bowl, add salt and stir in grated cheese and milk. Pour over onions, decorate with chopped tomato and mushrooms, if desired, and bake in a pre-heated moderately hot oven for fifteen to twenty minutes.

Individual Fruit Tarts

Juicy fruit pies can be a disaster on a picnic but, if made by the following method, they can be transported safely and easily. Quantities given allow for twelve individual tarts.

Ingredients

6 oz flour   1 packet 'Quick-jel'
3 oz margarine   small carton of cream (optional)
1 egg (beaten)
½ to ¾ lb stewed fruit *or* one medium sized can tinned fruit

You will need *either* a twelve-hole individual bun tray (deep) *or*, preferably, twelve individual foil dishes in which the tarts can be carried.

Method

Make pastry as in recipe on page 9 (mince pie recipe) using the above quantities and a beaten egg instead of water. Grease dishes and line with pastry, lightly pricking with a fork and bake in a moderately hot oven for fifteen minutes. Turn out onto a wire rack to cool. When cold, fill cases three-quarters full with fruit. Make up 'Quick-jel' as directed on the packet and spoon into cases until it just covers the fruit. Return tarts to cases to take to picnic. A small carton of cream may also be taken and a blob placed on each tart before eating.

Church Fetes

As you drive through the country in the summer it sometimes seems as if every tree has sprouted the same, or at least similar, strange new foliage. Half-way up a trunk of a beech by the side of the road, or hanging from a strategic branch of an oak are the notices:

'St Pancras and All Cherubs: Garden Party at the Vicarage': 'Passing-Soon-cum-Little-Worth Church Fete on the Recreation Ground': followed in every case, because we are all realists, by the message: 'In the Village Hall if wet'.

Summer is the season of church fêtes and coffee mornings. If sometimes there do not seem enough Saturdays to go round we do the best we can and, with a certain amount of planning and much goodwill, manage to buy our jam from St Gertrude and our cakes from Little-Mallow-in-the-Marsh. Meanwhile back in the parish, everyone has been busy: baking, boiling, brewing to provide goodies for the various stalls and the following recipes are offered in the hope that they might suggest some new ideas or at least remind you of old ones. Everyone buys homemade jam at fêtes but, as everyone also makes their own, it is the more unusual that go first, such as

Rose Petal Jam (called by children 'Fairies' jam')

Ingredients

1 lb rose petals, preferably red
8 oz sugar

8 oz honey
4 tablespoons water

Method

Collect rose petals as they are about to fall. (They can be kept, until you have collected enough, by placing them in an opaque container, sprinkling with a few drops of lemon juice and covering. Alternatively, they can be put in a deep freeze.) Wash petals and place in preserving pan with other ingredients. Simmer over low heat until sugar is dissolved. Bring to boil and boil hard until setting point is reached. (To test for this, place a small amount on a cold saucer. When cool it will set on the surface and wrinkle up if pushed with a spoon handle.) Cool slightly and pour into warm jars. Seal when cold. These quantities make approximately 1½ lb of jam.

Gooseberry and Strawberry *approximately 5 lb*

Ingredients

1½ lb gooseberries
1½ lb strawberries

3 lb preserving sugar
¼ pint water

Method

Top and tail gooseberries and hull strawberries. Wash, then place gooseberries in water in preserving pan and just bring to boil. Simmer until tender and add strawberries. Simmer for 5 minutes, add sugar and simmer until dissolved. Then boil hard until setting point is reached. (For setting point, see Rose Petal Jam, above.) Remove scum, cool slightly and pour into warm jars. Seal when cold.
(N.B. It is notoriously difficult to get Strawberry Jam to set. The addition of gooseberries not only solves this problem; it also provides a certain welcome tartness to the product.)

Hedgerow Jam *approximately 6 lb*

For sale in summer this has to be made the previous autumn but as it keeps well and sells, if anything, even better, we make no apology for including it here.

Ingredients

½ lb rosehips
½ lb rowanberries
½ lb sloes
½ lb haws
1 lb blackberries

1 lb elderberries
¼ lb hazel nuts
1 lb crab apples
4 lb sugar (appprox.)

Method

Wash all fruit. Core and chop crab apples, chop hazel nuts. Place hips, haws, rowanberries, sloes and crab apples in preserving pan. Cover with water and simmer until tender. Put through sieve to remove liquid, weigh pulp and return to pan. Add blackberries, elderberries and hazel nuts. Simmer for ¼ hour, then add sugar: the weight of the pulp, plus 2 lb. Simmer until sugar dissolves, then boil hard until setting point (see Rose Petal Jam, page 38) is reached. Cool slightly, pour into warm jars and seal when cold.

Green Tomato Jam

Like hedgerow jam, this is made the previous autumn and is a welcome alternative for anyone who does not care for chutney, but is faced with bushels of unripened tomatoes.

Ingredients

4 lbs tomatoes
3 lbs preserving sugar

Flavouring: cloves or ginger or lemon to taste

Method

Chop tomatoes, place in preserving pan and bring gently to the boil. Add sugar and flavouring: either a few cloves or a small piece of whole ginger (or 2 oz ground ginger) or the grated rind of a lemon (or a few drops lemon essence). Boil fast for about 20 minutes. Test for setting (see Rose Petal Jam, page 38). Cool slightly, pour into jars and seal when cold.

Chutneys are also popular and the great advantage of the following recipe is that you do not have to spend hours in the kitchen on a hot summer's day, bringing things to the boil.

Uncooked Rhubarb Chutney

Ingredients

4 lbs rhubarb
2 lbs onions
1 lb currants
1 lb raisins
1 lb sugar

1 level tablespoon ground ginger
1 tablespoon mustard
1 teaspoon salt
½ teaspoon cayenne pepper
1 pint vinegar

Method

Chop rhubarb, onions, currants and raisins finely, or put through mincer. Add other ingredients and leave to stand for a day or so. Taste, and add more spice if required.

The cake stall is a money spinner at the church fête and the following recipes can also be used to supply the tea tent.

Victoria Sponge

Ingredients

2 eggs
their weight in each of the following:
margarine
sugar
flour (remember to weigh the flour before you beat the eggs!)
a pinch of salt

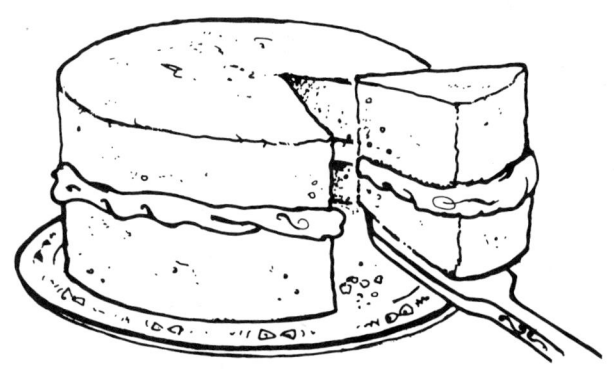

Method

Beat the eggs well and cream together margarine and sugar. Beat in the eggs, a half at a time. Fold in sifted flour and salt. Put mixture into two greased 7 inch tins and cook for 15 to 25 minutes in a moderate oven. Turn onto wire rack to cool. When completely cold spread a layer of jam on one sponge and sandwich together with the other.

The above ingredients and method can be used for small cakes baked in paper cases. When cold decorate with icing (see mince pie recipe, page 9) and glacé cherries, sugar strands or hundreds and thousands. Alternatively, bake in a swiss roll tin, cutting into squares when cold and decorate. 1 oz cocoa powder or a few drops of cochineal or other colouring may be added to the mixture to make it more decorative. If you don't mix the colouring evenly when adding, this gives a marble effect.

Rock Cakes (very suitable for St Peter's-tide!)

Ingredients

¾ lb self-raising flour
4 oz currants
3 oz margarine
3 oz sugar
1 oz mixed peel

1 egg
about ¼ pint milk
1 teaspoon baking powder
pinch of grated nutmeg

Method

Sieve flour into basin, adding baking powder. Rub in margarine lightly with fingertips. Add the dry ingredients and nutmeg. Stir in well-beaten egg, add milk, a little at a time. Do not make mixture too moist. Put in small heaps on a greased baking sheet and cook in a hot oven for 15 to 20 minutes.

Flapjacks

Ingredients

8 oz butter
8 oz demerara sugar
12 oz porage oats (9 oz oats, 3 oz Muesli base plus a few sultanas makes an exciting variation)

Method

Melt butter, stir in sugar and oats. Cook for a few minutes, stirring well. Spoon into a flat tin, well greased and lined and bake in a moderate oven till golden brown. Before quite cool cut into squares. Store in an airtight tin.

Irish Cake (see St Patrick, page 65)

Double the quantities for this recipe and bake in rectangular tins. Cut into oblong slices and serve with the teas.

Sardine Sandwiches

A large number of these can be made from the Biblical seven loaves and a few small fish: greatly appreciated by multitudes.

Ingredients

7 loaves of thin-sliced bread
9 tins of sardines
butter or margarine

Method

Mash up sardines and spread generously on the bread. Cut off sandwich crusts and cut each one in two diagonally.

And for the sweet stall:

Peppermint Creams

Ingredients

1 lb icing sugar
3 drops oil of peppermint
white of two medium eggs
green colouring (optional)

Method

Sieve icing sugar to remove all lumps. Whip egg whites with a fork until frothy. Add to icing sugar a bit at a time, stirring well. Add peppermint oil and colouring. Using your hands, mix to a smooth stiff paste. If mixture seems too dry and a few drops of water. Sprinkle board with icing sugar and roll out mixture to ½ inch in thickness. Cut into small rounds and leave overnight on a tray to set properly.

Fudge

Ingredients

1 large tin sweetened condensed milk
1 lb demerara sugar
¼ lb butter

Method

Place ingredients in saucepan and cook until the sugar has dissolved and the mixture boils. Remove from heat and beat well. Pour into a well-buttered tin. When cool, cut into squares.
Chocolate, walnuts, or vanilla flavouring may be added if desired.

7. Michaelmas

Michaelmas Goose

Not many people nowadays eat roast goose on the 29th September, the feast of St Michael and All Angels, and probably fewer still know how the custom originated. Dr Brewer, as one might expect, offers an ingenious theory in his 'Dictionary of Phrase and Fable'.

On her way to Tilbury, on the 29th September, 1588, Queen Elizabeth I dined with Sir Neville Umfreyville on two fine geese. She had just tossed off a bumper of Burgundy, giving as the toast: 'Destruction to the Spanish Armada!' when news came of its defeat. The Queen demanded a second bumper declaring, 'Henceforth shall a goose commemorate this great victory!'

This tale, says Brewer solemnly — although one can almost see his wink — is marred by the awkward circumstance that the thanksgiving sermon for the victory was preached at St Paul's on the 20th August and the fleet dispersed by the winds in July.

In fact it seems that geese were commonly eaten at Michaelmas as long ago as the fifteenth century — probably because a goose frequently formed part of the rent for that quarter. Perhaps we could give a nod to the old custom, without going all the way, by using one of the following recipes.

Mock Goose (with lentils) *serves four*

Ingredients

1 lb lentils
1 large onion
1 large cooking apple
4 rashers bacon

2 oz dripping
mixed herbs
pepper
salt

Method

Peel and chop onion and apple, removing core of latter. Boil with lentils and dripping in just under two pints of water (the apple will add moisture) until lentils are tender (about half to three-quarters of an hour) or pressure cook, following instructions. Add pepper, salt, and herbs, and turn into a baking dish, shaping as much like a goose as possible. Cover with bacon rashers and cook in hot oven or under grill until bacon is cooked. Serve with savoury sauce or 14 oz tin of tomatoes.

Stuffed Vegetable Marrow (Seasonal; also called 'mock goose')

Ingredients

1 vegetable marrow

for stuffing:

2 large onions
1 teaspoon dried sage
1 breakfastcup soft breadcrumbs
or use packet sage and onion stuffing

1 oz butter
1 egg
pepper and salt to taste

Method

Peel marrow, cut in half lengthwise and take out seeds. Peel onions, boil for five minutes and chop finely, or mince. Mix with breadcrumbs, sage, butter, egg and seasoning, *or* make up packet of stuffing, following instructions. Fill marrow with mixture, put both halves together, brush with butter and bake in a moderately hot oven until tender (about a half to three-quarters of an hour).

Angel Cake

The roast goose of Michaelmas, it seems, is really a secular bird, connected with the quarter day, 29th September, rather than with the saint and his angelic companions. Some Christian families mark the day by having angel cake at teatime, whatever they may have for dinner.

Ingredients

for cake:

3 oz twice sieved plain flour
6 oz sugar — granulated will do
6 egg whites
1 level teaspoon cream of tartar
½ teaspoon vanilla essence
¼ teaspoon almond essence
pinch of salt

for glacé icing:

8 oz icing sugar
2 tablespoons warm water
a few drops of lemon essence

Method

Beat egg whites with salt until stiff. Add cream of tartar and beat until mixture stands up in peaks. Add 4 oz of the sugar and vanilla and almond essence. Sieve flour twice and mix with remaining 2 oz sugar. Fold gently into rest of mixture. Put into a NON-greased cake tin and cut through several times with a knife to let out air, otherwise holes will appear in the cake when cooked. Bake in a slow pre-heated oven (electricity 275°F 140C, gas mark 1) for half-an-hour. Turn up heat (electricity 325°F 170C, gas mark 3) for a further half hour. Turn upside down onto a wire tray and ease out of tin when cold. Ice with glacé icing.

To make icing: Crush and sieve icing sugar. Mix with enough warm liquid to make the icing coat the back of a spoon without running off too freely. Beat well and add a few drops lemon essence. Pour over cake. The icing should dry with a shine, but will lose this if over-heated.

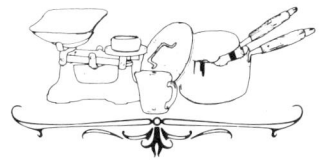

8. Harvest Supper

The Harvest Festival is not strictly speaking part of the Church's Year, but in this increasingly industrial age it seems to have come to stay. It was as recently — in terms of Church history — as 1843 that Mr Hawker of Morwenstow, in Cornwall, invited his parishioners on a Sunday in late summer to take their communion 'in the bread of the new corn' — a custom he had taken from the moribund Lammas, or 'loaf-mass' festival at the beginning of August. Thirty years later there was hardly a church in England which did not hold its Harvest Festival. No particular Sunday is set apart for this and it can take place any week from September to late October, although the later date is not popular with the flower arrangers whose job it is to decorate the church. More recently many churches have adopted the custom of holding a Harvest Supper, usually on the Monday following the festival service in the church. These no longer take place in the farmers' barns when the corn has been safely gathered in but in the Church Hall and the women of the parish are expected to provide the eats. The menu can vary from a buffet with everyone bringing something so that all may have enough, to a two- or three-course sit down meal. For the latter, a vegetable or harvest stew would be appropriate.

Harvest Stew

Ingredients

root vegetables such as potatoes, carrots, swedes, parsnips, turnips — allow ½ lb of each per person, proportionately less for larger numbers

½ medium courgette per person, *or* equivalent amount of vegetable marrow
1 medium onion to every four persons
dripping
seasoning
mixed herbs
stock
flour

Method

Chop all vegetables and fry onions until tender. Add courgettes and marrow, then other vegetables and cook for a few minutes. Add stock to cover, seasoning and herbs to taste, and bring to boil. The marrow or courgette will provide moisture so be careful with the stock. Simmer, or cook in a slow oven until vegetables are tender. Thicken with flour if necessary. Other vegetables, such as tomatoes, celery and mushrooms can be used as well. If preferred, the whole can be rubbed through a sieve or put into a blender and made into a thick soup.

Soup or stew, slices of homemade bread (see Lenten Lunches, page 19) or homemade bread rolls will be a good accompaniment.

Bread Rolls

Ingredients

3 lb strong plain flour
3 teaspoons salt
1 oz yeast

1 ½ pints milk and water mixed
1 teaspoon clear honey
1 oz lard

Method

Mix salt with flour and rub in fat. Put honey and yeast together and leave till liquid and add lukewarm water. Pour into a 'well' in the flour and leave till spongey. Mix and knead for about five minutes, or until dough comes away from bowl. Cover and leave to prove in a warm place until dough doubles in size. Shape into rolls and cook for fifteen minutes in a hot oven. If tops of rolls are rubbed with a butter paper just before cooking this improves the appearance.

For the sweet course we suggest the following is both seasonal and appropriate.

Mother Eve's Pudding (or Paradise Pudding)

If you'd have a good pudding, observe what you're taught
Take twopennyworth of eggs when twelve for the groat
And of the same fruit that Eve had once chosen
Well pared and well chopped at least half a dozen.
Six ounces of bread (let your man eat the crust)
The crumbs must be grated as fine as the dust.
Six ounces of raisins from the stones you must sort
Lest they break all your teeth and spoil all your sport.
Five ounces of sugar won't make it too sweet,
Some salt and some nutmeg will make it complete.
Three hours let it boil without hurry or flutter,
And then serve it up without sugar or butter.
Adam tasted the pudding, twas wonderfully nice,
So Eve cut her husband another good slice.

Those of us brought up in the tradition that it was the tomato, or 'love-apple' that Eve chose will have a curious pudding. Perhaps we had better stick to Bramleys.

Ingredients

6 eggs
6 apples
6 oz breadcrumbs
6 oz seedless raisins

5 oz sugar
salt
nutmeg to taste

Method

Peel and slice apples and beat eggs. Mix all ingredients together and put into a buttered basin, cover with greaseproof paper and pudding cloth and steam for three hours. Or you can cheat a little and beat the sugar into 5 oz of butter, add the bread-crumbs (or 5 oz of flour) and eggs and pour over the apples in a well-buttered pie dish and bake till cooked.

Some versions of this recipe add:

'Take four ounces of suet, well chopped it must be
The mixture now ready, quite good you'll agree'

while others don't think it is complete until

'To this you can add, if you're willing and handy,
Some good lemon peel and a glass of good brandy.'

It was this last one, incidentally, that Adam preferred.

A large round pumpkin seems to be as much a part of Harvest Festival as it is of 'Cinderella' and pies, even if they cannot be made from the pumpkins given to the church, provide a very suitable contribution to the Harvest Supper. As some churches auction their harvest fruit and vegetables you may in any case find yourself persuaded into buying a large pumpkin in the name of charity and because 'it will be just the thing for Hallowe'en.' Well, maybe, but what do you do with all that bland, soft pumpkin flesh when it has been scooped out to make the lantern? It is criminal to throw it away, when more than half the world is starving, and you paid so much for it anyway. The answer, of course, is pumpkin pie — Waterloo County, Ontario style.

Pumpkin Pie

Ingredients for one 8 inch pie

for pastry: 4 oz flour
2 oz margarine
pinch of salt

for filling: 2 cups (8 oz) mashed pumpkin
1 cup sugar
1 cup sour cream
3 eggs, well-beaten
2 tablespoons molasses
2 tablespoons melted butter
1 teaspoon vanilla
½ teaspoon each, nutmeg and cinnamon
1/8 teaspoon cloves

Method

Make pastry as on page 9 (mince pie recipe) using the above quantities and line a well-greased 8 inch pie dish. Mix all other ingredients well together and turn into unbaked pastry case and cook in a moderate oven for 45 minutes, or until well set.
This is real Mennonite style Pumpkin Pie, not the poor, restaurant style substitute.

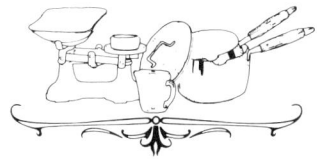

9. Parish Catering

Stewardship Suppers

The Carnival and Harvest Suppers are, of course, spring and autumn events. The Stewardship Supper (with its annual follow-up) can take place at any time in the year, but the recipes given for other occasions (vegetable soup, page 47, hot or cold beef, page 16 and Mardi Gras salad, page 16) can be used for this as well. However, if you want something different, Quiches are popular and easy to make. They can be served at a sit down supper or cut up into manageable portions for a buffet-style meal. Either everyone on the catering committee undertakes to make one or two, which spreads the load and provides variety, or one or two people can make a few at a time, freezing until required. It is best to make the pastry in separate batches, freezing until needed if necessary, but the basic filling can be made in bulk, with different garnishes added. The following recipe is for one 8 inch quiche serving six people. Quantities for the filling can be doubled, trebled, etc for larger numbers.

Quiche

Ingredients

for pastry:
4 oz flour
2 oz margarine
pinch of salt

for basic filling:
4 eggs
¾ pint single cream, or milk
½ teaspoon salt

cayenne pepper and grated nutmeg to taste

garnish suggestions:
3 rashers bacon, grilled and chopped *or*
8 oz grated cheese *or*
8 oz onions, finely chopped and fried till brown *or*
5 oz shelled and chopped raw shrimps *or*
4 oz chopped mushrooms *or*
4 medium tomatoes chopped

(smaller quantities of cheese, onion, tomato and mushroom can be added to any other combination of ingredients)

Method

Make pastry as on page 9 (mince pie recipe). Roll out and put into well-greased tin(s). Mix ingredients for basic filling and beat lightly. Add garnishes as required and pour into tins within about ¼ inch of the top. Bake in a moderate oven until filling is set (about 30-40 minutes). Serve hot or cold.

Either way, they are excellent with salads. When serving salads to large numbers it is a good idea to put the ingredients in separate bowls as well as in a big dish of mixed salad, and to provide a large jug of salad cream (page 35) so that people can mix their own, according to taste.

Lemon Mousse

For the sweet course lemon mousse offers a possibly welcome alternative to the pancakes (page 17) and apple pudding (page 48) which are almost mandatory for Carnival and Harvest Suppers. The following recipe serves twenty. Increase quantities in proportion for larger numbers.

Ingredients

7 lemons
14 eggs, separated
6 oz granulated sugar

1¾ oz gelatine
1 pint double cream

Method

Grate the yellow part of the lemon rinds and set aside. Squeeze the juice and mix with gelatine. Stand for ten minutes. Mix egg yolks with grated rind and sugar and beat hard until mixture is light and lemon-coloured. Heat lemon juice and gelatine over low heat until gelatine dissolves, then stir into yolk mixture. Beat cream until thick, and fold into mousse mixture; whip egg whites until stiff and fold into mousse mixture too. Pour into large serving bowls or individual cups. If wished garnish with whipped cream (one pint for twenty people) and almonds before serving.

The Parish Breakfast

Another tradition in the making is the increasingly popular Parish Breakfast after the early communion on Sunday mornings. As cooking facilities can be limited in Parish Halls, bacon and egg flans can be made at home beforehand and either served cold, or warmed up if facilities allow. This also enables the cooks to come to the service and to take their full part in the fellowship.

Bacon and Egg Flan   *serves six. Increase quantities as required.*

Ingredients

for pastry: 6 oz flour
3 oz margarine
pinch of salt

for filling: 4 rashers bacon
4 eggs
½ teaspoon mixed herbs
salt and pepper to taste

Method

Make pastry as on page 9 (mince pie recipe) and line greased 8 inch tin. Cut rashers into small pieces and spread over pastry. Beat eggs and stir in herbs and seasoning. Cook for 30-40 minutes in a hot oven.

A Continental style breakfast of rolls and coffee is simpler and the bread recipes on pages 19 and 47 can be used. But why not make croissants? The crescent shape does not appear to have any religious significance and in any case they will presumably be blessed by the grace said beforehand.

Croissants

Ingredients *for one dozen. Increase quantities as required.*

½ lb plain flour
1 level teaspoon salt
½ oz yeast
1 oz caster sugar (optional, but at least one teaspoon is required)
4 oz butter or margarine
¼ pint cold milk
a little beaten egg and milk for the glaze

Method

Mix yeast with a teaspoonful of the caster sugar until if liquifies. Sift the flour and salt into a large mixing bowl and mix in the rest of the sugar, if used. Add the milk to the yeast mixture, strain this into the flour and mix to a stiffish dough. Turn onto a floured board and knead thoroughly till smooth. Roll out the dough into a strip ½ an inch thick, about 12 inches long, 7 inches wide, being careful to keep the corners as square as possible. Cut the butter or margarine into slices and lay them over the middle of the strip of dough, leaving a small space at each side. Next fold one end of the strip over half the butter and the other end over the other half so that the two ends meet in the middle. Now fold the dough in half as if you were shutting a book. With the dough in front of you as if you were about to open the 'book' roll it out again into a strip and repeat the folding process. Repeat the whole rolling and folding process twice more, then wrap the dough loosely in a floured cloth and leave it to rise in a warm room for half-an-hour. Roll the dough out into a rectangle measuring about 11 inches by 17 inches. Cut into six 5½ inch squares. Cut each square in half diagonally, making twelve triangles. Roll up each triangle, beginning with the longest side and working to the point. Moisten the point of each triangle with a little egg and milk so that it holds the roll firmly together. Bend each roll into a crescent shape and lay it on a lightly greased baking tray. Cover with a cloth and leave in a warm place to prove. (This will take half to three-quarters of an hour.) Be careful not to overheat at this stage. They are ready for baking when they seem light and puffy. Cook them in the top of a hot oven for seven or eight minutes, then take them out and brush lightly and quickly with the beaten egg and milk. Reduce heat slightly and continue to bake for a further three or four minutes.

For the coffee to go with them the following rough guide is useful.
1 level desertspoon instant coffee to a pint of water makes enough for five large cups, milk extra. Allow one pint of milk to every six to twelve cups.

For tea allow one tea bag to every two people. With larger numbers you will need proportionately fewer tea bags. Allow one pint of milk to every fifteen to twenty cups of tea. With a large boiler and a good supply of tea bags and instant coffee you can keep brewing indefinitely and if you have a tin of powdered milk in reserve you should be able to feed, perhaps not the five thousand, but at least as many as are likely to turn up, however unexpected.

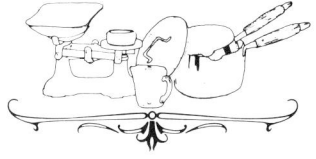

10. Special Sundays and Other Feasts

Bible Sunday

As more and more Sundays are allocated to a certain subject or a good cause, so there are more chances for cooks to establish new traditions to stand alongside those from the past. For Bible Sunday (the second in Advent) we suggest

Old Testament, or Scripture, Cake

Ingredients

4½ cups 1 Kings, Chapter 4, verse 22
½ lb Judges, Chapter 5, verse 25
2 cups Jeremiah, Chapter 6, verse 20
2 cups Nahum, Chapter 3, verse 12
2 cups 1 Samuel, Chapter 30, verse 12
2 cups Numbers, Chapter 17, verse 8
1½ cups Judges, Chapter 4, verse 19
6 Jeremiah, Chapter 17, verse 11
2 teaspoons 1 Samuel, Chapter 14, verse 25
2 teaspoons Amos, Chapter 4, verse 5
1 pinch Leviticus, Chapter 2, verse 13
to taste 2 Chronicles, Chapter 9, verse 9

Method

Proverbs, Chapter 23, verse 14

The key to this recipe is given on page 68.

New Year's Day

Although the Scots might not agree with us, New Year's Day is not a religious festival and the Church in general appears to have no special recipes connected with it, but in the sixteenth century godparents living in Coventry gave their godchildren special cakes on this day. They were triangular in shape, and the three points were said to represent the church spires in the city and/or the Trinity. If this custom were revived, and became universal, it might even be transferred to Trinity Sunday, which seems to be singularly lacking in traditional recipes of its own.

Coventry Godcakes

Ingredients

13 oz puff pastry (frozen will do very well)
8 oz mincemeat
granulated sugar to dust

Method

Thaw, and roll out pastry thinly, to an oblong. Cut into twelve 4 inch squares and cut across to form twenty-four triangles. Place a teaspoon of mincemeat in the centre of twelve of them. Dampen the edges and place the remaining triangles on top. Seal well. Brush with water and sprinkle thickly with sugar. Bake in a hot oven for twenty minutes.

Patronal Festival

It depends, of course, on the dedication of your particular saint whether your patronal festival takes the form of a revel on the village green with ice-cream and cool drinks or folk-dancing in the village hall with hot sausage rolls and coffee, but in either case Devonshire Revel Buns would be an appropriate addition to the menu.

Devonshire Revel Buns

Ingredients

1 lb plain flour
¼ of a level teaspoon salt
4 oz butter
¼ level teaspoon powdered saffron (optional)
¼ pint tepid milk
½ oz fresh yeast, or 2 level teaspoons dried yeast

1 small egg, beaten
¼ pint single cream
pinch ground cinnamon
4 oz currants
6 oz caster sugar

Method

Sift flour and salt and rub in butter. Add saffron, if used, to warmed milk. Stand for ten minutes, then strain. Cream fresh yeast with tepid liquid, or, if dried yeast is used, stir one level teaspoon caster sugar into tepid liquid, then sprinkle yeast on top and leave for ten minutes, or until frothy. Make a well in the flour, pour in the yeast liquid, cream, egg and cinnamon. Mix to a soft dough. Cover, leave in a warm place for forty-five minutes, until almost double in bulk. Knead fruit and sugar into risen mixture, shaping into twelve buns. Put on greased baking sheet and leave in a warm place for fifteen minutes. Bake in centre of pre-heated moderately hot oven for thirty minutes. Cool. Eat on the same day.

Traditionally, each bun was baked on a sycamore leaf: we don't know why.

Overseas Sunday

It is a good idea, when arranging a special 'do' in connection with the Church's work overseas to provide at least some dishes made according to recipes from faraway places. Thanks to the increased speed of transport and perhaps to the demand of people from those places now settled in England creating the supply, it is easier than it used to be to obtain some of the more exotic ingredients. Where this is impossible a more humble, home-grown version can be used instead.

Callaloo

Calloloo is to Trinidad what the joint-and-two-veg is to England. It is traditionally cooked on Sundays, possibly because of the time it takes. We must remember that church is over by half-past eight in the morning and one has the rest of the day in which to cook and enjoy callaloo *and* go to the beach.

Ingredients *for about four*

about 1 lb dasheen leaves (substitute spinach for these)
8 ochres (obtainable from the vegetable shelves of larger supermarkets)
1 to 3 small crabs (tinned crabs or fish can be used)
1 ham bone
2 cups water
1 tablespoon butter
1 onion
1 green hot pepper (the small hot pepper, NOT the large 'sweet' one)
thyme, chives, garlic to taste

Method

Wash and cut up vegetables EXCEPT the pepper. This must ON NO ACCOUNT be punctured or the dish will scald your scalp off. Scald crabs and clean them, if fresh. Put all solid ingredients, except butter, into a saucepan, add boiling water and simmer with the pepper on top until everything is tender (except the ham bone of course) and soft enough to mash easily — about half to three-quarters of an hour. Remove the pepper and ham bone, add butter and whisk or blend the mixture. (It is better to take out the crabs before putting through blender.) The result is a curious-looking green mush with pink ochre seeds floating in it and large chunks of crab, still in the shell, lurking in the depths. You can remove the crab from the shell if you want to. Adjust seasoning and serve either as a purée vegetable or as soup.

Samosas

These small savoury pastries are served for afternoon tea in India, but are equally suitable for a finger buffet supper. They seem to be small Cornish pasties in exotic Eastern dress.

Ingredients *for 32-36 samosas*

for pastry:

1½ cups plain flour
¾ teaspoon salt
1 tablespoon oil
½ cup warm water

for filling:

1 tablespoon oil
1 clove garlic, finely chopped *or* 2 teaspoons minced garlic
1 teaspoon finely chopped fresh ginger *or* 1 heaped teaspoon ground ginger
2 medium onions, finely chopped
2 teaspoons curry powder
½ teaspoon salt
1 tablespoon vinegar or lemon juice
8 oz minced lean lamb or beef
½ cup hot water
2 tablespoons chopped fresh coriander or mint leaves
oil for deep frying

Method

Pastry: Sieve flour and salt into a bowl, add oil and warm water, mixing thoroughly until ingredients are combined, adding a little more water if necessary. Knead for about ten minutes, or until dough is elastic. Cover and set aside while preparing filling.

Filling: Heat oil in a saucepan and fry half the onion until it is soft, with garlic and ginger. Add curry powder, salt and vinegar and mix well. Add minced meat and fry over a high heat, stirring continuously until meat changes colour. Turn down heat and add hot water. Cover and cook till meat is tender and all the liquid absorbed, stirring frequently towards the end of cooking time to prevent meat sticking. Sprinkle with chopped coriander, or mint, remove from heat and allow to cool. Mix in rest of chopped onion. Form small pieces of dough into balls and roll out thinly into squares, approximately 4½ inches, on a floured board. Cut each square in half diagonally and place a teaspoon of filling on one side of each triangle and brush edges with water. Fold over and press together firmly. Heat oil in a deep pan and fry a few at a time until golden brown on both sides. Drain on absorbent paper and serve hot.

Samosas can be kept successfully until needed if they are frozen *separately* on trays after filling and then packed in bags for storing in the freezer. Thaw before frying.

Confirmation Sunday

A bishop once said that an essential qualification for the job was the ability to consume the varied and strange dishes that were offered at the parish feasts after confirmation services and the institutions of vicars. Perhaps *Bishop's Bread* was concocted by our American cousins to be served on similar occasions in their Episcopalian Church. The following is one of the various recipes, all delicious, that go by that name. Why not give the Bishop a pleasant surprise on your next Confirmation Sunday?

Bishop's Bread

Ingredients

4 eggs, separated
1 cup sugar (American 'cup' = 8 fluid ounces)
1 teaspoon vanilla
1 cup sifted flour
2 teaspoons baking powder
1/8 teaspoon salt
1 cup almonds, blanched and chopped
1 cup raisins
confectioners' sugar (the equivalent of this can be made by putting 1 cup granulated sugar, 2 teaspoons plain flour *or* 1 teaspoon cornflour into blender for one minute).

Method

Separate eggs, blanch and chop almonds. Beat egg yolks until light and lemon-coloured, add sugar and beat well. Sift dry ingredients together and stir into egg mixture. Add nuts and raisins. Fold in the stiffly-beaten egg whites. Pour into oblong greased baking tin and bake in a moderate oven for twenty minutes or in a hot oven for ten minutes. While still hot, cover with confectioners' sugar and cut into squares. Serve at once. If wanted for an after-church function the mixture can be prepared beforehand and baked quickly in a hot oven while the congregation are coming out.

Any Sunday

Of course it can be said that every Sunday is a special day, and it can be a busy one for the cook, with the Sunday dinner being perhaps the only meal in the week shared at leisure by the whole family. The joint can usually look after itself in the oven, and the following is a quick and easy pudding, as its name implies.

After Church Pudding

Ingredients

2 tablespoon flour
1 tablespoon sugar
1 tablespoon chopped suet (packet suet will do)

1 egg
½ pint milk

Method

Mix together flour, sugar and chopped suet. Add beaten egg to mixture. Pour on boiling milk and mix well. Bake in moderate oven for half-an-hour. Serve with jam, treacle or stewed fruit.

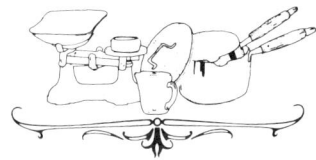

11. Saints' Days

It seems a pity that, apart from the special fare provided by some University colleges in honour of their patron saints, there are no traditional dishes which immediately spring to mind in connection with any one saint: perhaps they were considered to have souls above such things. Let us remedy this defect and begin with a universally beloved saint whose day surely everyone knows — the 14th February.

Saint Valentine

It appears that there were probably two rather obscure Valentines. One, at least, was a bishop and was martyred on the 14th February under the Emperor Claudius in the year 270. It so happened that this date more or less coincided with the rather dubious pagan festival of Lupercalia at which couples were paired off according to the lots they had drawn. The Church, as in other instances, unable to suppress this pagan custom gave it the blessing of a saint and of nature itself — birds were popularly supposed to choose their mates and begin to build their nests on this date.

Dr Brewer, not surprisingly, has a different theory. 'Valentine', he says, is a corruption of the word 'galatin', a lover (or 'dangler') and was chosen as the sweethearts' saint because of his name. This seems a little unlikely and anyway, matters not at all to those who send and receive Valentines, or to those girls who make Valentine biscuits. These are simple and fun to make and are at least appreciated by those boys who find them slipped into their desks at school — if this custom still prevails.

Valentine Biscuits

Ingredients

8 oz plain flour
4 oz margarine
2 oz icing sugar
3 teaspoons baking powder
½ teaspoon salt

milk to mix
a little red jam
four 1½" strips angelica
a small heart-shaped biscuit cutter will be needed

Method

Place dry ingredients into a bowl and rub in margarine with fingertips until the mixture is like breadcrumbs. Mix in the milk until a firm dough is formed. Roll out on a floured board and cut into an even number of heart shapes. Place on a greased baking sheet and cook for ten to fifteen minutes in a slow oven. Put on wire trays to cool, then sandwich pairs together with red jam. While biscuits are baking, cut angelica into thin strips, one for each biscuit. Make one end pointed, keeping the bits cut off. Sift icing sugar and mix with a few drops of warm water to form a stiff paste. Spread over top of biscuits and decorate with angelica arrows using the two bits cut off to make the points for the fins.

We know of a person who served the following dish to her family on a cold day in February without realising the significance of what she was doing until she happened to glance at the calendar.

Roast Sheeps' Hearts

Ingredients

2 sheeps' hearts
2 oz forcemeat
dripping

Method

Wash hearts thoroughly, remove tubes and stuff with forcemeat. Sew up opening, cover hearts with dripping and put into a roasting tin, cover with cooking foil. Cook in a moderately hot oven for one to one and a half hours, basting frequently.

Saint Denis

St Denis — the French very sensibly abbreviated the name of Dionysius, the first Bishop of Paris — appears to have been martyred, by decapitation, in either the first or the third century and very little else seems to be known about him. According to tradition, he carried his head for six miles, deliberately putting it down on the spot where the cathedral dedicated to his name now stands. This story probably originated from an ancient painting depicting his martyrdom with a headless trunk: then, so that he might be recognised, the artist painted in the head, between the martyr's hands. Although he is the patron saint of Paris there are Celtic connections and at St Denis, in Cornwall, the tartlets more generally known as 'Maid-of-Honour Tarts' were called after him. Whether or not they were served on St Denis day — the 9th of October — we do not know.

Saint Denis Tartlets

Ingredients

for short pastry: 6 oz flour
2 oz butter

for filling: 2 oz caster sugar
1 whole egg
1 egg yolk
2 oz ground almonds
1 level tablespoon cornflour
a little vanilla essence
raspberry jam
a little icing sugar

Method

Make pastry according to recipe on page 9 (mince pie recipe), and line fifteen patty tins with it. Cream butter and sugar until thick. Beat in egg yolks, one at a time. Add almond, cornflour and vanilla. Lastly fold in stiffly whisked egg white. Place small teaspoon raspberry jam at the bottom of each tart and fill with mixture. Make a cross with two strips of pastry on the top of each tart and bake in a hot oven for 15-20 minutes. Dust with icing sugar.

Saint Luke

'Run, run, as fast as you can—
You can't catch me, I'm the gingerbread man.'

Has this old rhyme, recently revived in children's books, any connections with the prodigal son?

In medieval times gingerbread men used to be distributed on the Sunday nearest to St Luke's day — the 18th of October — to symbolise the feast of the Prodigal Son, one of the two parables told only by St Luke. Ginger, said to be the oldest spice in the world, has medicinal properties which could have been known to Luke, the 'beloved physician' and this may be the reason for making these biscuit men of gingerbread. Later they gave place to ginger or brandy snaps and their religious significance was forgotten.

Gingerbread Biscuits

Ingredients

¼ lb flour
2 oz sugar
2 oz butter
1 teaspoon ginger

½ teaspoon baking powder
a little beaten egg
currants
glacé cherries

Method

Put flour, sugar, ginger and baking powder into a bowl. Rub in butter with fingertips until mixture is like fine breadcrumbs. Stir in a little beaten egg with a knife until a stiff dough is formed. Roll out on a floured board and cut into shapes. Decorate with currants for eyes and buttons, and with slices of glacé cherry for the mouth. Place on a greased baking sheet and cook in a moderate oven until firm to touch — about ten minutes.

Brandy Snaps

Ingredients

4 oz golden syrup
4 oz sugar

4 oz flour
4 oz butter

Method

Heat sugar, butter and syrup in a saucepan until the sugar is dissolved, but do not let it boil. Stir in flour. Place a teaspoonful of the mixture for each snap on a greased baking sheet, allowing plenty of room for them to spread. Bake in a pre-heated slow oven until a golden colour — about fifteen minues. Allow to stand for about a minute before lifting off sheet and curling round the handle of a wooden spoon to shape.

Patron Saints of the British Isles

It is easy to find recipes for the patron saint of the British Isles. If the following are not traditional, they ought to be.

Recently there have been misguided attempts to substitute the daffodil for the leek as the Welsh emblem, presumably on the grounds that, as a mere vegetable the latter was not fit to associate with the English rose and the Scots thistle. Luckily they have not succeeded and the leek remains the proud emblem of the Welsh as it was long before the days of Henry V. According to Shakespeare, the Welshman, Fluellen, reminded the King that he, too, was born in Wales: 'and I do believe your majesty takes no scorn to wear the leek upon St Tavy's day.' (Henry V, Act iv, Scene 7.) The tradition goes back to the legendary days when David, a Welsh resistance leader, according to some chroniclers, the uncle of King Arthur, ordered the Welsh to wear leeks in their caps to distinguish them in battle. They were victorious and commemorated their success by wearing the leek on the 1st of March, the anniversary of their defeat of the Saxons.

The best way for Welshmen to observe the custom nowadays would be to have leek soup for dinner on St David's day — the 1st of March.

Leek Soup *serves four*

Ingredients

4 good sized leeks
2 pints stock or water
1 stick white celery (optional)
1 large potato (optional)

1 oz grated cheese
½ oz dripping
salt \} to taste
pepper

Method

Chop vegetables (omit potatoes if a thinner soup is preferred). Melt dripping in pan and cook vegetables gently for about ten minutes without browning. Add seasoning and stock or water, bring to boil and simmer until vegetables are tender, or cook in pressure cooker, following instructions. If preferred, rub through sieve or put in blender. Serve grated cheese separately, to be added at table.

Question: 'What is called after a country and an animal although it has nothing to do with either?'
Answer: 'Welsh rabbit'.
Of course spelling the second word 'rare-bit' makes more sense and, as for the first, well, it gives as good an excuse as any for serving it on St David's day.

Welsh Rarebit *for two or three people*

Ingredients

¼ lb grated Cheddar cheese
1 egg (optional)
2 tablespoons milk

1 tablespoon mustard or Worcester sauce
½ oz butter or margarine
a slice of toast for each person

Method

Melt butter or margarine in small pan. Add other ingredients and cook slowly until mixture comes to the boil and is thick and creamy. Pour onto buttered toast and either serve at once, or brown under grill or in oven for a few minutes.

We do not have to look very far for a suitable dish to serve on St Patrick's day, the 17th of March.

Irish Stew

Ingredients

1 lb neck of mutton
2 lb potatoes
2 onions
½ pint stock or water

2 oz pearl barley
1 teaspoon salt
pepper to taste

Method

Trim meat and cut into small pieces, and slice onions, place in a saucepan with stock or water and bring to boil. Remove scum and simmer for half-an-hour. Add potatoes cut into cubes, pearl barley and seasoning. Simmer until potatoes are soft and most of the liquid absorbed — for about half an hour — with the lid tightly closed. If preferred, cook in a casserole in the oven.

Irish Cake

This economical cake, recommended for church fête teas (Summer Days, page 41) makes a good family cake as well. It is not for nothing that it is sometimes called a 'cut-and-come-again' cake.

Ingredients

1 lb flour
½ lb dripping or packet suet
½ lb raisins
½ lb currants
2 oz mixed peel, cut thin

½ lb sugar
½ teaspoon bicarbonate of soda
½ teaspoon cream of tartar
½ pint of milk

Method

Sift flour into basin and rub in dripping or suet. Add raisins, currants, peel and sugar. Mix. Mix bicarbonate of soda and cream of tartar in a jug and pour milk over. Beat in egg and moisten cake mixture with liquid, adding more milk if required, as it should be quite moist. Put into a greased 8 inch round cake tin and bake in a slow oven for 2¼ hours.

Roast beef and Yorkshire pudding would seem the obvious choice for St George's day but G.K. Chesterton wrote:
'St George he was for England
And knew what England means,
Unless you give him bacon
You mustn't give him beans.'
This does not mean fried rashers and baked beans but the traditional Sum-

mer dish of boiled bacon with broad beans and, thanks to deep-freezing, it is perfectly possible to serve it on the 23rd of April.

Boiled Bacon and Beans *serves four*

Ingredients

3-4 lb bacon joint, recommended for boiling
cloves
tablespoon demerara sugar *or*
tablespoon honey *or*
dried breadcrumbs
1 lb broad beans (when shelled)

Method

Soak bacon, if smoked, for a few hours in cold water. Bring to boil in fresh water, skim, add three of four cloves and demerara sugar (unless using later for roasting) and simmer for twenty minutes to the pound, and twenty minutes over. Or cook in pressure cooker, following instructions. Skin if necessary and sprinkle with breadcrumbs. If preferred joint can now be baked in a hot oven for a further fifteen minutes. Alternatively, score the fat with a sharp knife after stripping skin, rub over with demerara sugar or honey and bake for fifteen minutes, basting with the liquor in which bacon was boiled. This can be served as a gravy with the meat.
Boil beans in a little salted water and serve with parsley sauce.

For anyone South of the Scottish border a recipe for haggis which begins 'Procure the large stomach-bag of a sheep' is more than a little daunting but perhaps we can acknowledge St Andrew — after all he wasn't a Scot himself — with an easier version. This is also a Scottish recipe, described as 'simpler haggis' and recommended for the bairns.

Simpler Scotch Haggis *serves four*

Ingredients

3 or 4 handfuls oatmeal
½ lb suet, minced fine *or* packet of suet
½ lb cold meat, minced

1 large onion
a little parsley
salt, pepper to taste

Method

Brown oatmeal in a hot oven — about twenty minutes. Mince suet, if necessary, meat, onion and parsley. Mix together with oatmeal and seasoning, moisten with a cupful of water, put in a closed pan and simmer until cooked — about two to three hours. If preferred, it may be cooked in a moderately hot oven in a casserole.

Oatmeal, of course, figures in many Scottish recipes.

Oatcake

Ingredients

4 oz fine oatmeal
4 oz coarse oatmeal } obtainable at Whole Food Stores
2½ oz dripping *or* lard
teaspoon salt
pinch of bicarbonate of soda
hot water

Method

Mix flour and oatmeal together and rub in fat. Add the soda and salt and mix to a dough with hot water. The dough should not be too dry. Sprinkle pastry board and dough with meal and roll out very thin. Cut into rounds or triangles. Bake in a moderate oven for about twenty minutes, turning them over half-way through.

And so, as we eat these oatcakes, spread with heather honey or Dundee marmalade, for tea on the 30th of November, we realise we have come to the end of another year in the Christian calendar, with its feasts, fasts and festivals. We have probably already been reminded by the collect for the Sunday-next-before-Advent ('Stir up Sunday') to make our Christmas puddings, so may we end with the rhyme taught to one of us by her grandmother, a good church woman and a wonderful cook?

'Stir up, O Lord, we beseech thee
The pudding in the pot —
And please see to it, O Lord,
That you make it nice and hot!'

APPENDIX

Key to Scripture Cake recipe on page 54.

Ingredients

And Solomon's provision for one day was thirty measures of fine *flour* (4½ cups)
She brought forth *butter* in a lordly dish (½ lb)
The *sweet cane* from a far country? (sugar) (2 cups)
All thy strongholds shall be like fig trees with first ripe *figs* (2 cups)
Two clusters of *raisins* (2 cups)
The rod of Aaron was budded . . . and yielded *almonds* (2 cups)
And she opened a bottle of *milk*, and gave him drink (1½ cups)
As a partridge sitteth on *eggs* and hatcheth them not (6)
And there was *honey* upon the ground (2 teaspoons)
And offer a sacrifice of thanksgiving with *leaven* (yeast, or baking powder, 2 teaspoons)
And every oblation . . . shalt thou season with *salt* (one pinch)
And of *spices* great abundance (to taste)

Method

Thou shalt *beat* him with the rod
Beat butter, sugar and honey to a cream. Add eggs, one at a time, still beating. Add raisins, figs (chopped) almonds (blanched and chopped) and beat again. Mix flour, spices, salt, yeast (or baking powder) and add to the other ingredients. Add milk. Bake in a slow oven for 1½-2 hours.

METRIC CONVERSION TABLE

Solid Measures

APPROXIMATE EQUIVALENTS

British	Metric
1 lb (16 oz)	450—500g
½ lb (8 oz)	225—250g
¼ lb (4 oz)	100—125g
1 oz	25g

Liquid Measures

APPROXIMATE EQUIVALENTS

British			Metric
1 quart = 2 pints	= 40 fl oz	=	1.1 litre
1 pint = 4 gills	= 20 fl oz	=	600 ml
½ pint = 2 gills or 1 cup	= 10 fl oz	=	300 ml
¼ pint = 8 tablespoons	= 5 fl oz	=	150 ml
1 tablespoon	= just over ½ fl oz	=	15 ml
1 dessertspoon	= ⅓ fl oz	=	10 ml
1 teaspoon	= 1/6 fl oz	=	5 ml

Temperature Equivalents for Oven Thermostat Markings

Degrees Fahrenheit	Gas Mark	degrees Centigrade	Heat of Oven
225	¼	*110*	Very cool
250	½	*120-130*	Very cool
275	1	*140*	Cool
300	2	*150*	Cool
325	3	*160-170*	Moderate
350	4	*180*	Moderate
375	5	*190*	Fairly hot
400	6	*200*	Fairly hot
425	7	*220*	Hot
450	8	*230*	Very hot
475	9	*240*	Very hot

Index of Recipes

After church pudding 59
Angel cake 45
Apple pudding (see Mother Eve's)
Arctic roll 13

Bacon and egg flan 52
Bishop's bread 58
Boiled bacon and beans 66
Brandy butter 13
Brandy snaps 63
Bread (homemade) 19
Bread rolls 47
Bread sauce 12
Brisket of beef 16

Callaloo (from Trinidad) 56
Celery, onion and apple stuffing 12
Cheese, egg and onion flan 37
Chestnut and sausagemeat stuffing 12
Christmas dinner menu 11
Christmas pudding (Queen Victoria's) 8
Chutney (uncooked rhubarb) 40
Coffee and tea 53
Coleslaw (and dressing) 35
Coventry Godcakes 55
Croissants 53
Curate's pudding 33
Curry pasties 36

Date pudding 22

Easter biscuits 29

Fastnachts 17
Fig pudding 25
Fish potato pie 24
Flapjacks 41
Fruit tarts (individual) 37
Frumenty 21
Fudge 42

Gingerbread biscuits 63
Gooseberry fool 32
Gooseberry mallow pie 31
Gooseberry and strawberry jam 38
Greek Easter cakes 28
Green tomato jam 39

Haggis (see Simpler Scotch Haggis)
Harvest stew 47
Hedgerow jam 39
Hot Cross buns 23

Irish cake 41 & 65
Irish stew 65

Leek soup 64
Lemon mousse 51
Lentils (Mock Goose) 44

Mardi Gras salad 16
Marrow, stuffed (Mock Goose) 44
Mince pies 9
Mother Eve's pudding 48
Mustard sauce 16

Oatcakes 67
Old Testament cake (see Scripture cake)

Pace eggs 26
Pancakes 17
Paschal (see Pace eggs)
Paskha 29
Peppermint creams 42
Pumpkin pie 49
Punch 10

Queen Victoria's Christmas pudding 8
Quiche 51

Revel buns (Devonshire) 55
Rhubarb (Dunfillan) 27
Roast sheeps' hearts 61
Rock cakes 41
Rose petal jam 38

Saint Denis tartlets 62
Salad cream 35
Samosas (from Sri Lanka) 57
Sardine sandwiches 42
Scripture cake 54
Simnel cake 21
Simpler Scotch haggis 66
Soufflés 31
Stuffed vegetable marrow 44

Tansy pudding (1 & 2) 27, 28

Valentine biscuits 61
Victoria sponge (and variations) 40

Welsh rarebit 64
White pot 32